Overcoming Doubt, Fear and Procrastination

Identifying the Symptoms, Overcoming the Obstacles

By Barbara Wright Sykes

COLLINS PUBLICATIONS
Chino Hills, CA 91709

Overcoming Doubt, Fear and Procrastination

Identifying the Symptoms, Overcoming the Obstacles

By Barbara Wright Sykes

Published by: COLLINS PUBLICATIONS
3233 Grand Avenue, Suite N-294
Chino Hills, CA 91709-1318

Cover Design by Ann Collins
Cover Art by Ken Clubb
Layout and Design by Ann Collins
a:/Prompt Business Support
Edited by: Laura Harrison-Tull
Katie Mead
Gail Blake-Smith

Copyright © 1996, by Barbara Wright Sykes
Printed in the United States of America

Publisher's Cataloging in Publication
(Prepared by Quality Books Inc.)

Wright Sykes, Barbara, 1947-
Overcoming Doubt, Fear and Procrastination: Identifying the
Symptoms, Overcoming the Obstacles /
by Barbara Wright Sykes.
p. cm.
Includes bibliographical references and index.
Preassigned LCCN: 96-084707
ISBN 0-9632857-7-7

1. Success--Psychological aspects. 2. Self-doubt. 3. Procrastination
4. Self-acceptance. 5. Fear of success. I. Title.

BF637.S8W75 1996   158.1
QBI96-30059

Table Of Contents

Table Of Illustrations

Warning—Disclaimer

This book is specifically written to provide information on identifying the symptoms and overcoming the obstacles associated with doubt, fear and procrastination. It is sold with the understanding that the author and the publisher are not licensed therapists, psychologists or clinicians. If psychological or other expert clinical assistance is required, the services of a competent professional should be sought.

Overcoming doubt, fear and procrastination is not an overnight process, and in some instances self-help may not be sufficient. It is the sole responsibility of the readers to determine to what extent they are experiencing these issues and take the necessary steps to achieve the desired results.

Extensive research, studies and interviews have been conducted to gather data and information on doubt, fear and procrastination. However, the author and publisher shall be held harmless with respect to the validity of statements made by, or on behalf of, those persons appearing in this book.

To protect the privacy and confidentiality of people involved in the various studies, and interviews, some names have been changed. References to people, places and things may be purely coincidental. However, some of the interviewees have chosen not to exercise their right to anonymity.

Acknowledgments

First and foremost, I give thanks to my Heavenly Father. A special thanks goes to Katie Mead and a:/Prompt Business Support; the library staff at Ontario South and Ontario Main; Tobin & Associates; and to my loving family for their support and understanding: Fletcher, Tiffany, Adrienne, Deitrich, Mattie, James, Percy, Nina, Shiam, Tony, Sylvia, Booker and Pearl.

I would like to express my gratitude to the many individuals who shared, contributed, supported and gave so unselfishly of themselves:

Nancy Aldredge
Pat Tobin
S. Barry Hamdani
Carlease Burke
Connie Amaden-Crawford
Dr. Cecil Whiting
Paul Aldredge
Gail Blake-Smith
John Clemons
Dr. Jane Myers Drew
Derek Scott
Nima Patel
Don Price
Jerrold Curry
Mary Kay Schreiber
Lisa Valore
Gail Taylor Walton
Pastor Dave Stoecklein
Roberta Pierce
Alice Wright
Dee Freeman
Herman Waer
Bill Daley
Dan Poynter
John Kremer
Warren George
Laura Harrison-Tull
Lisa Gordon
Leilani Armstrong
Keith and Candy Stump

DEDICATED TO....

Three of the most phenomenal women:

To my mother Mattie, who gave me the special gift of life, and taught me how to overcome doubt, fear and procrastination, and to believe in myself.

In loving memory to a special angel Bessie Randolph, whose spirit still lives on through the outstanding contribution and generosity of her beautiful daughter—Pat Tobin.

They say it takes a village to raise a child. Each person's love, devotion and care has a significant affect on the growth and development of that child. I have been blessed. My life has been touched by a person who has all of those qualities and more—Roxanna Sanders.

With love...

Barbara

Introduction

There are three common enemies that will rob you of achieving your success: ***Doubt, Fear and Procrastination***. Why do we allow them to have so much power? How can we determine when they are taking place? Are the symptoms always apparent? Can we overcome the obstacles caused by doubt, fear and procrastination, and move on to success?

These questions have been a source of concern for many people. Some have sought counseling in hopes that deep introspection would reveal the symptoms, and allow them to conquer the obstacles. Discouraging as it may seem, one must never give up hope. In the midst of the frustration, you may find yourself asking: Is it really possible to achieve success in spite of the obstacles?

There is good news. The answer is—**Yes!** However, it will require some of your precious time. You will need time to first identify the symptoms—your symptoms, and second, to overcome the obstacles that have been holding you back. It is important to note that the emphasis is on *your* symptoms. Do not make the mistake of assuming that your symptoms are akin to someone else's, and therefore the same principles apply. Everyone has his or her own cross to bear. Depending on your life experience you may respond differently from your peers to the symptoms that cause you doubt, fear and procrastination.

You must keep in mind that your particular situation is unique. It is unique because you are the one experiencing doubt, fear and procrastination; unique because your level of experience and resources may be different, and you alone have the sole responsibility to solve the problem. Therefore, you must consider to what extent you will apply certain principles. We are all different in our own right, and what works for someone else may not necessarily work for you.

It is vitally important that you get in touch with your inner being. People around you, in your sphere of influence, will assign their values and belief systems to you. If you are weak and dependent on what others think of you, you will fall prey to their beliefs, and subscribe to their value system. Consequently, you will find yourself being influenced to apply pressure on yourself to meet their expectations when, in fact, your chief concern should be that of meeting your own expectations.

Doubt, fear and procrastination are interesting elements of human behavior. Fear knows no limits. There are a number of fears that people have to face, ranging anywhere from self-accomplishment to the fear of snakes. Some fears tend to be more damaging than others. There are many theories on how to handle fear. How you handle fear will be dependent upon the degree of anxiety the fear is causing you. What should be of concern is the issue of degree. If your fears render you helpless, or cause you to become incapacitated, then clinical help is strongly suggested. It should be noted that the majority of individuals do not suffer from fear to that extent. Self-introspection can often render a cure. In the following chapters you will be exposed to various self-help principles and theories.

Doubt is a unique emotional element in the grand scheme of the big three—doubt, fear and procrastination. Doubt is a close relative of fear. Some argue that one comes before the other. Some say it is the doubt that causes them to have fear; others maintain that it is the fear that causes them to have doubt. It is similar to the age-old question: "Which came first, the chicken or the egg?"

In a recent study it was revealed that doubt is the second stage of the process which fear created. There is no argument that doubt is a major roadblock to success! Once fear has been introduced, it leaves a stop sign in its place called doubt. Doubt causes you to second guess your ability to move forward, to accomplish a goal, and to enjoy your heart's desire. It becomes the obstacle between you and your success.

When doubt is present, you start to question issues and situations with respect to *your* ability to succeed: Can I really do this? What will people think? What if I fail? I've never done this before! They will never loan *me* the money! Once the emotional roadblock is in place, your natural reaction is to retreat. You either do nothing or give a series of useless excuses as to why you cannot move forward and accomplish your goal, ultimately causing you to procrastinate. When you fall prey to procrastination, you give yourself permission to buy into a negative thought process. You begin to think to yourself: *It's just not in the cards for me, and no matter what I do, success is simply out of reach!*

The truth is, your attitude should be one of positive thinking. Your self-talk should be: "Yes, I have some concerns regarding the situation, circumstance, venture, and opportunity; *nevertheless*, I am worthy, qualified and able to achieve success; nothing or no one is going to stop me!"

What happens to the value of procrastination with this type of attitude? It loses its power; it ceases to have any value with respect to you and your abilities. Caution must be exercised. It is imperative that you stay clear of others who are negative. They will try to convince you that the positive principles you have adopted are easy in theory and difficult in practice. Not so, when you learn the keys to overcoming doubt, fear and procrastination.

Successful individuals are not exempt from doubt, fear and procrastination, they simply respond differently. In the ensuing chapters a number of successful individuals have shared their experiences, secrets, theories and principles. Your window of opportunity allowing you to examine their secrets to overcoming doubt, fear and procrastination lies ahead. Yours is only to turn the page!

Accepting the Truth

1

Boy, do I need this book! Overcoming Doubt, Fear and Procrastination; doesn't that sound familiar? I often ask myself, "Why can't I change my ways?" I know my life would be better if I could just get myself together. Then there are times when I feel that I am together; and still other times when I feel that I am falling apart at the seams.

Poor Me, Poor Me—Why Me?

You know, it's funny. I can be having a good day; then all of a sudden, I'll get a call from someone, hear something, or see something that will remind me of a task or assignment I should have done, but didn't for one reason or another. What's so aggravating is that I can't tell you why I didn't follow through. I guess I am just not ready to deal with it.

Nevertheless, I have been extremely busy. People just don't seem to understand the enormous responsibility I have. Times are really hard these days, and there just doesn't seem to be enough time to get things done.

Some people never seem to have a care in the world. Could it be that they don't have to face the challenges of doubt, fear and procrastination? That's nonsense—no one is perfect. What's wrong with me?

I've been under a great deal of stress; things aren't going well for me at work. My boss gave me the time and motion study to complete for the Sorrenson account, and I didn't even get it done! When the alarm went off this morning, I just couldn't go into work and tell him I haven't completed the project. I can hear him now: "Frank, what happened? I gave you this project over two weeks ago. You've had more than enough time!"

Thank goodness I am no longer married to Katherine; she always talked to me as if I were her son, instead of her husband. We have been divorced for two years and I am so glad she wasn't there when I called my boss this morning. I know her like a book; she would have started in with one of her infamous lectures: "Frank, that's what's wrong with you—you never complete anything. You have no sense of urgency...no respect for time. All you do is procrastinate! That's why we're in the condition we're in today. You will never keep a decent job!"

A man has his pride, and he just can't let a woman run over him. Knowing me, I would have retaliated by saying, "Procrastinate! Is that what I've been doing, Katherine? *Procrastinating?*"

I must admit we had some good times. Katherine did do something with her life. She's Senior Vice President of Wallingford & Tate, an advertising agency in New York. Wow! I'd better be careful—for a minute there I almost thought I missed her.

I went to the bookstore this afternoon and was surprised to see Hugh Sterling, one of my old high school classmates. It was really good to see him. He looked healthy and prosperous. I remember that no one ever thought he would turn out to be much of anything, not to mention graduating from high school. Would you believe he has his own business? We graduated at the same time, so he's got to be at least my age. He has a few strands of gray near the temples, but looks fit as a fiddle—not even a beer belly!

Hugh spotted me and began to ask questions about what I've been doing with my life, so I became self-conscious and tucked my stomach in. I hoped he wouldn't notice that I had gained a considerable amount of weight since high school. It's not my fault. I don't have time to go to the gym.

I didn't have the heart to tell him what I've *really* been doing, so I quickly excused myself by saying I was late for an executive meeting. Why did I feel the need to lie? Who am I kidding? I wish I had an executive *anything* to go to! If things hadn't worked out the way they have, I'd be in his shoes. I'd be successful and have my own business, too.

I know why I lied; I was afraid that compared to him, he would see me as a failure. As I stood there assessing my behavior, he became aware of the book I was holding and said, "*Overcoming Doubt, Fear and Procrastination*. I used to really struggle with that problem before I was willing to accept the truth and do something about it."

Hugh spoke with such seriousness in his voice. It had the severity of those who speak of recovering from alcohol abuse or drug addiction. I was paralyzed as I stood there with a blank expression on my face. It was as though he could see right through me.

He looked me straight in the eyes as he continued to speak, "I didn't get my life together until I worked through those issues. Once you are aware of the symptoms, you can overcome the obstacles. Everything started to change for the better when I changed my attitude about life. Soon after that I went into business, got married, and the rest, as they say, is *history*."

I never would have guessed that I would run into Hugh Sterling—at a bookstore, of all places. It has been said that things happen for a reason. I've got to be honest, Hugh's testimony was extremely sobering. When he left, I could still hear his voice repeating over and over in my mind...."I used to really struggle with that problem before I was willing to accept the truth and do something about it." As I stood in line to purchase the book, I realized that I *am* making a conscious decision to accept the truth. I am going to overcome *doubt, fear and procrastination.*

The Truth Shall Set You Free!

Accepting the truth is therapeutic and refreshing. Change and healing will not take place until you are willing to shed old habits and behaviors. The birth of this process comes through a total commitment to the truth.

Taking an assessment of behavioral patterns that are counterproductive, and in some cases destructive, can be painful. The pain is more severe when someone else points out your flaws. First of all, it doesn't feel good to hear, and it can be extremely uncomfortable.

Any character flaw or trait that doesn't lend itself to a positive personal or public image tends to get masked or tucked away and, in most cases, denied. The thought of not being perfect, or at least being viewed as not perfect, is too much for some individuals to cope with, thus creating a false or pretentious view of themselves.

People who suffer from this problem tend to find comfort in lies, putting on airs, and hiding behind a false persona. It is not that they are unaware of the situation; it is just too painful for them to accept the truth and initiate change. Some have operated in this mode for so long that it has become totally acceptable behavior—at least in their eyes.

Nevertheless, in order to become successful in your personal and professional life, you must find that place of comfort that will allow you the strength to face the issues and accept the truth—no matter how painful.

Frank knew he had a problem. However, it made him feel more comfortable to deny the truth regarding certain issues. In the beginning you get a sense that he was on the threshold of getting himself together. This was evident when he accepted the fact that the quality of his life would have major improvements if he would change his behavioral patterns.

In a rare moment, you saw Frank admiring Katherine's accomplishments. He knew that his level of success was being sabotaged by his constant need to put things off. For the first time, Frank seriously considered the fact that Katherine was right in her assessment of his tendency to procrastinate. It became painfully clear to him that his inability to stop procrastinating was his chief downfall. He realized that both his personal life and his professional life were being greatly affected by his behavior.

In an effort to save face and to protect his ego, Frank found comfort in lying to Hugh Sterling about his accomplishments since high school. The fear of being thought of as a failure was his prime motivating factor. Hugh was enormously successful and Frank couldn't bear being thought of as anything less than successful.

Frank's tendency to procrastinate had some underlying roots spawned from the fear of tackling issues head on. He simply didn't feel competent, and therefore set himself up for ultimate failure.

When Frank was faced with a situation where he needed assistance, he wouldn't ask for help. His ego would not allow him to stretch himself and say that he had some concerns and needed help. He felt that he would be viewed as incompetent. Rather than face the facts, he found solace in putting things off, which resulted in feelings of guilt. Frank's acceptance of the truth and his sincere desire to initiate change was the beginning of the healing process.

When faced with the dilemma, Frank should have analyzed the situation in order to solve the problem. The example on the next page demonstrates Frank assessing the problem and applying techniques to solve the problem.

Living in an imperfect world we must face a number of challenges. We must decide where to place value, and how to prioritize the things that truly have the greatest significance.

Coping with our emotions can be difficult. A number of issues play havoc with our decision-making process. Our frame of reference to life experiences will have influence on our socio-economic status and cause us to behave differently to various emotional stimuli. People in our immediate sphere of influence will shape and mold how we perform in a given situation. The greater the value we place on another individual, whether real or perceived, will often affect how we interact toward them.

When you find your behavior causing you to feel uncomfortable in a given situation, you must step back and analyze why you are responding abnormally. Do you feel threatened or intimidated by an individual? Are you feeling inadequate or inferior with respect to your ability to perform? Do you feel that your knowledge and skill level are not on par with others in your-rank and file? Is your ego at risk? You will have to assess the causes in order to rectify the problem.

Frank Works Through The Problem

Problem:	I didn't complete the project assigned.
Why:	I put it off and ran out of time. When I did decide to start, it was too complicated.
Causes: Doubt Fear Procrastination	I doubted that I could successfully complete the project and meet the deadline. When I realized how difficult it was and that I needed help, I began to panic. I put the project off; I felt I had sufficient time.
Outcome:	I let my boss down. I lied to him about being sick, rather than tell him the truth.
Problem Solving:	When I received the project I should have: 1) reviewed it. 2) allocated sufficient time. 3) outlined the steps needed to successfully complete it on time. 4) realized I needed further assistance, and informed my superior.

Frank experienced a whole range of emotions. In helping him get to the root of his problem, he conducted an exercise entitled, *Food for Thought.* He simply utilized a series of questions to determine what he was really feeling. This simple process allowed him to understand the underlying reasons for his behavior and put into place a method for change. An adaptation of Frank's "food for thought" principle appears on the page 21.

For this method to be effective you must emotionally separate yourself from the situation. This will allow you to analyze all the elements of the picture with a much clearer focus. You must be willing to be totally open and honest with yourself. Once you have achieved that status you can concentrate on what emotional stimuli are evoking these responses. Next, you can weigh the issues and apply the proper steps to correct your behavior.

Fear plays an enormous part in procrastination. Identifying your fears and acknowledging the underlying causes associated with your behavior is a healthy step toward recovery.

Food For Thought

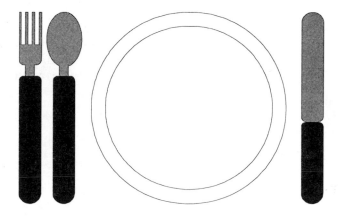

- How important is it to protect my ego?
- More importantly, when is it appropriate to do so?
- Whose opinion really matters, anyway?
- Is it important that I make the other person feel good about me?
- Or, should I strive to feel good about myself—no mater what the cost?
- Are there risks associated with telling the truth?
- What will be the outcome?
- Do I really procrastinate?
- Do I have a reason to feel guilty?
- Do I fear responsibility?

Name That Fear

2

Fear is said to be agitation or dismay in the anticipation of, or in the presence of danger. Fear can possess both posi- tive and negative attributes. We all fear something or someone. However, we must identify the cause and symptoms before we can overcome the obstacles.

Identifying The Symptoms.

As children we are taught to look to our parents for protection when we are frightened. We find a safe haven in the arms of our mother and father. The role of a parent is to comfort the child by gently pointing out that there is nothing to be afraid of. Because the parent is near, the child knows that he is safe, in spite of what is perceived as dangerous.

The parent explains the nature of the fear in an effort to convince the child that what is causing the fear is unfounded. There really isn't a monster or a ghost in the room; it's simply a shadow on the wall caused by a tree blowing in the night wind.

The identification of the cause [the tree] has reas- sured the youngster that there is no danger; the tree is harmless and his fear of danger is totally unnecessary. The child now has a process to follow when overcoming this particular fear. In addition, the child has a general frame of reference to assist him in working through the obstacle of fear.

Thus, the next time this incident occurs, the child will understand that the shadow on the wall is just the tree blowing in the wind. Consequently, there is no present danger, and therefore no cause for alarm.

> *Thou shalt not be afraid for the*
> *terror by night...*
> *—Psalms 91:5*

If we are taught these reasoning skills to identify fear and its causes, and how to overcome the obstacles, then why is it that we as adults cannot transfer this simple lesson into our adult life? We allow ourselves to become paralyzed by fear. In most cases, if we stopped to analyze the circumstances, we would find that we have the solution to eliminate the problem.

Perhaps we feel that the process used by children is too simplistic, and because we are adults, with adult problems, there must be a more sophisticated solution. In the case of extreme fear—incapacitating fear where therapy is needed—the answer is not that simple. However, in day-to-day situations, we can employ the process of thinking through the problem causing the fear. One of the more effective ways is to utilize the five-step approach.

The five-step approach allows you to dissect your fears through identifying the symptoms logically and realistically, thus providing the platform to implement an effective method for overcoming the obstacles. The following steps will assist you in working through the problems associated with doubt, fear and procrastination:

The Five-Step Approach

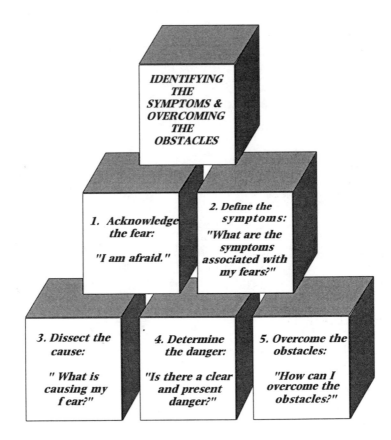

Step 1:   Acknowledge The Fear:

You must first recognize that you are experiencing fear—you are afraid. Do not deny the fact that these feelings exist. It is extremely healthy when you can get in touch with your feelings. There is nothing wrong with having these feelings. The problem occurs when you allow them to incapacitate you. Some people experience fear to such a degree that it renders them helpless. They are in a temporary holding pattern, unable to move forward, for fear of danger or loss of security.

Be not afraid of sudden fear....   —Proverbs 3:25
I sought the Lord, and he heard me, and delivered
me from all my fears.   —Psalms 34:4

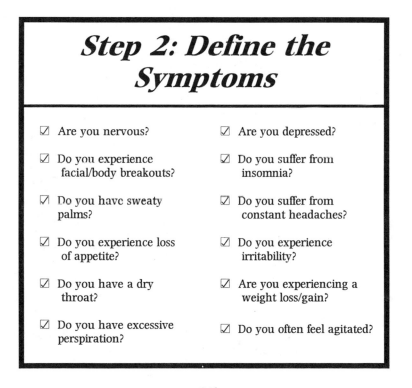

Step 2: Define the Symptoms

☑ Are you nervous?

☑ Do you experience facial/body breakouts?

☑ Do you have sweaty palms?

☑ Do you experience loss of appetite?

☑ Do you have a dry throat?

☑ Do you have excessive perspiration?

☑ Are you depressed?

☑ Do you suffer from insomnia?

☑ Do you suffer from constant headaches?

☑ Do you experience irritability?

☑ Are you experiencing a weight loss/gain?

☑ Do you often feel agitated?

25

Overcoming Doubt, Fear and Procrastination

Step 2: Define The symptoms:
Procrastination is a by-product of fear. When you find yourself procrastinating, more than likely you are doing so because of a fear-based stimuli. For the moment, you may not be aware of what is happening to you. However, you are aware that your behavior is out of the norm and you are uncomfortable. You refuse to go forward and complete a task or project. You find it very difficult to concentrate. You tend to avoid individuals associated with the situation or circumstance that is causing you the discomfort. You find yourself more at ease avoiding the issue. The more you exercise this behavior the more *your* personal symptoms begin to surface. Once you have defined these symptoms (the sweaty palms, nervous anxiety, avoidance, etc.), it is easy to recognize when you are in the throes of fear.

Step 3: Identify The Cause:
Assess the cause of the fear. Initiating a cure for the problem takes more than just knowing that you are afraid. Having a clear understanding of the cause of your fear will help you to work through the issue. When you examine the issues associated with the problem, it tends to break down the power or hold that fear places on you. In many cases, you begin to see that what is causing your distress is not as bad as you imagined.

A prime example is the child being afraid of the shadow on the wall created by the trees blowing in the night wind. A simple explanation by the parent relinquished the child's fear of shadows. The child understood that there was no cause for alarm and he could return to a safe night's sleep. More importantly, whenever the situation arose, the child had a frame of reference which allowed him to mentally accept the fact that the shadow posed no threat to his safety.

In essence, as adults we must dissect the cause of our fears in much the same way. We need to understand the cause, know that we can do something about it, and not allow it to pose a threat. Once the cause is uncovered, we can then examine avenues of resolution, and these resolutions can be applied when we respond to these kinds of fear-based stimuli.

Step 4: Is There A Clear And Present Danger? Is My Perception Accurate?

Ask yourself, is there really a clear and present danger, and if so, what is the danger? Is your perception of the danger real and accurate? Understanding the elements of the situation with respect to being a potential threat to your safety allows you to break down the fear into real or imagined danger. Many times your perception of the danger prompts you to place undue value on the cause, thus preventing you from moving forward. At this point, you allow fear to take over. It is simply a matter of your taking control and assessing the situation clearly. Identifying that there is no real and present danger to your safety or social status will allow you to function and avoid procrastination brought on by fear.

There were they in great fear, where no fear was....
—Psalms 53:5

Step 5: How Can I Overcome The Obstacles?

Finally, how can you overcome these obstacles, and what are your options? Attitude reconditioning is the key to overcoming the roadblocks. You must implement techniques to help you eliminate fear-based stimuli through attitude reconditioning. Steps one through four are the platform needed to begin to institute attitude reconditioning. The only way to move past fear is to first acknowledge it, understand the symptoms, dissect the cause, and determine whether there is a real or imagined threat or danger.

There are a number of methods you can utilize to help you overcome the obstacle of fear. Some may be successfully implemented on your own, depending upon the degree of fear and anxiety you are experiencing, while others, where fear has rendered you incapacitated, will require clinical assistance. In this chapter, clinical psychologist Dr. Cecil Whiting further defines fear and gives suggestions on different techniques for fear resolution through attitude reconditioning.

Fearfulness and trembling are come upon me, and horror hath overwhelmed me. And I said, Oh that I had wings like a dove for then would I fly away, and be at rest. —*Psalms 55:5,6*

Fear and Fear Resolution

Dr. Cecil Whiting comments on fear: If you wanted a single definition of fear, I would say nervousness caused by noxious environmental stimuli. A fear reaction is more physiological. The blood flow in your body under conditions of fear tends to change. The head is a peripheral area and blood leaves the head first. It leaves all peripheral areas and moves toward the center of the body.

Blood vessels constrict. That's why your hands become cold when you experience fear. This is an indicator of how much stress you are under. If your hands are cold, there is generally a little bit of stress.

As the blood moves and shunts toward the center of the body, the heartbeat becomes stronger and sometimes faster. That happens to keep the blood flowing, and to keep energy going to the vital parts of the body. Vision becomes acute so that you can see any-thing; any movement that happens around you—you can see it. Your hearing becomes acute so that you can hear a pin drop.

During this process, the body is changing physio-logically, and it is on an emergency status. Pain recep-tors are no longer functioning. For example, if you are running from a saber-toothed tiger and step on a thorn, you won't feel the thorn because your pain receptors have shut off. You don't have time for that; your feet have to keep moving. It's quite possible for you to have a fairly good injury to your foot and not feel the pain until you have escaped the danger.

As you are running, most of the things that hap-pen are automatic. The breathing becomes deep and profound so that you are assimilating enough oxygen to keep the body moving. You will have sufficient blood supply for those parts of your body that are prepared for what is called *fight or flight*. This philosophy came from William James around the year 1876.

How do you overcome doubt, fear and procrastination?
There are probably a number of methods for overcoming doubt, fear and procrastination. For myself, one of the most effective methods is what Donald Meichembaum and Aaron T. Beck call *Cognitive Behav-ior Therapy*. They have developed a clinical aspect to something that sounds very much like Norman Vincent Peale's, *Positive Thinking*. Mohammed Ali implemented the theory prior to Meichembaum and Beck.

When Ali says, "I am the greatest," he is actu-ally confirming his belief in himself, and he begins to be-lieve it. By the constant repetition of the statement, he is changing or modifying the tape that plays in his mind.

As he modifies the tape he becomes that which he says he is.

One of the things I have done with patients in the past is to have them recite what it is they want to be. We measure a day. If a waking day (an active day) is ten hours, you have sixty seconds per minute, and sixty minutes per hour; that means you have thirty-six hundred seconds an hour. If you are repeating anything that takes three seconds, that means you could repeat it twelve hundred times in an hour. To avoid jeopardizing the perception of others with regard to your sanity, when you are in public you'll have to say it in your mind. When you are alone, sometimes it's best to say it out loud, repeating it several times, changing the emphasis on different syllables. If you were to say to yourself that you are having a very good day today, you would start by saying:

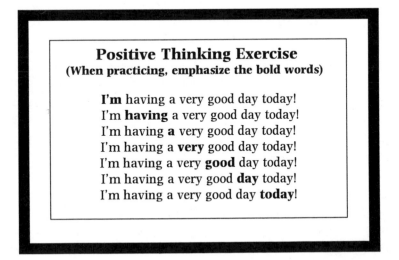

Positive Thinking Exercise
(When practicing, emphasize the bold words)

I'm having a very good day today!
I'm **having** a very good day today!
I'm having **a** very good day today!
I'm having a **very** good day today!
I'm having a very **good** day today!
I'm having a very good **day** today!
I'm having a very good day **today**!

You would repeat it indefinitely, and eventually, you would have *a very good day!* This is very similar to the way that Meichembaum and Beck have constructed

Cognitive Behavior Therapy. As long as a person becomes repetitive in terms of verbalizing a feeling or emotion, that emotion becomes part of how he responds. The major hurdle is getting the patient to resist saying, "I can't lie to myself." That's something that the person has to overcome. It's not considered to be a lie. It is a wish more than anything else.

The methods that are most effective with people are the methods that tend to be very natural. People almost stumble on them by serendipity. When you can come up with something that seems to work for you, that is a natural method; you have done it without professional consultation.

How to find a good therapist.

I think part of finding the right professional is finding one who uses or advocates methods similar to the methods you have already been using and have had some success with. Psycho-analytical methods tend to go against the grain of logic. Sometimes it's very difficult to do. I'm not very psycho-analytically oriented. It almost goes against the natural way things are. But there is an old method that tends to be somewhat psychoanalytic called *introspection;* no one uses it as much in therapeutic settings now. Part of the reason is that introspection is a function of an old non-scientific system called *structuralism.* As psychology became more scientific, non-scientific methods were no longer practiced.

Structured introspection should be looked at more closely today—getting people in touch with how they are feeling at this particular point. People who are afraid of heights tend to avoid examining their feelings. Those people have a tendency not to experience what stress is like. For example, I am a little bit afraid of heights.

31

I avoid the stress of heights, because subconsciously my hands begin to sweat, I become shaky and feel discomfort in my abdomen—that's stress.

If you experience that feeling, and you are going into an area other than heights, for instance, seeking a job, or starting a business, and you have those same feelings that you had with the fear of heights, then you know that you are experiencing perhaps one of the big three—doubt, fear and procrastination. Colombo used to say on TV that he was afraid of heights. People would say, "How much afraid of heights are you?" He would say, "I don't like being this tall!"

How can you cope with doubt, fear and procrastination?
Fear engenders doubt, and doubt will make you procrastinate to the extent that you are going through that process. The one thing that has to happen is that the methods you use for fear of heights are the methods you use to overcome doubt, fear and procrastination.

Here is another example: In terms of starting a new business, or going into a new venture, the feelings I have are very much the same as the feelings I have when I am confronted with heights. So to avoid that, "I won't do something." That's when doubt, fear and procrastination become incapacitating and unhealthy.

The methods that are most effective in getting a person ready to cope are breathing and deep muscle relaxation. It is very natural, and people do natural things. When something is difficult, you hear people sigh. That is natural and it relaxes them so they can start moving on.

Other methods include throwing oneself into "the lion's den," and the structured relaxation technique. Joseph Wolpe developed a method called *systematic desensitization*. This could be a deep muscle relaxation;

however, it briefly exposes a person to the noxious stimuli, or the fear in small increments while the person learns to relax.

If you have taught a person to relax and then you expose them to whatever they are fearful of, such as heights, on a hierarchical level that person can do almost anything. If I were working with a person who is afraid of heights, I would bring in a stepladder. I would ask the person to relax. I would probably hold the person's hand to determine whether or not that person was relaxed as he began to ascend the ladder. If the hand tightened, I would say there was too much tension and would tell the person to come down. Then I would ask that person to relax again, and take one step at a time until he felt comfortable.

Another classic example: There was a college student who could not study because she stayed awake all night, fearful that snakes would slither under her door. She was terrified of snakes, even though there were no snakes in the area. That's an extreme phobia (fear), so she went to a therapist. He took her through a hierarchy; at first he exposed her to a picture of a snake. The picture was too far away for her to distinguish that it was a snake. He told her to hold his hand and take one step closer. She responded by saying, "Oh, that's a snake!" Then he held the picture far away again and asked, "Now can you see the snake?" She said, "No." Then she was able to move one step closer to the picture. For the final lesson, after about six weeks of therapy, he took a baby boa constrictor and let her hold it and said, "let it wrap around your arm."

The one physiological reaction to fear that most people have is tension. Now, if you are tense and there is a boa constrictor on your arm, the snake may break your arm. Basically, putting a boa constrictor around the patient's arm and telling her to relax meant that she had to relax and remain relaxed. She knew this and it was planned beforehand. She was treated successfully for her fear of snakes.

Fear of being berated

It depends if you're being berated on a personal level or on your ability to succeed. There is a difference. There's a joke: A guy goes to a doctor and the doctor says, "You're stupid." The guy says, "I want a second opinion." The doctor says, "you're ugly, too!" Humorous as it is, that shows an example of someone being berated personally. If someone says you don't know what you are doing, you need to consider the credibility of the person. Is he someone you should listen to, or is he a person who doesn't know what he is talking about? This information is needed to decide whether or not the criticism is valid.

Fear of loneliness

Those individuals need to be given assurance that there is no need to be alone. If a person has what is called a borderline personality, he will leave home, rather than stay in a house alone. Giving him the idea that there are substitutes to being lonely, such as speaking to people on the phone, will help him build healthy relationships with people on the phone, even if he becomes lonely. The idea is for that person to be personable enough and friendly enough so that he or she is never really alone.

Fear of rejection

You can overcome rejection with your own personalized focus group. If you have others that accept you and support you, then the fear of rejection will have less of an impact.

The fear of death

One of the ways to overcome the fear of death is denial. That denial is what makes teenagers more reckless than older people. They have not faced their own mortality. As a result, they don't fear death. Consequently, denial is part of the process to get you to overcome the fear of death. My perception of death is a little different. I have a pseudo-metaphysical perception of death, and it has helped me.

For a person who thinks about death constantly, I would suggest *thought stoppage.* Every time a person who has a fear of death thinks about it, particularly if that person is alone, he can yell, "Stop!" He should do it very loudly, shake his head, and go on about his business. Now, if he does this every time it comes into his mind, eventually it will go away, because he has successfully blocked it.

The fear of flying

I think this has to be overcome in a group. For a person who is going into business or who is already in a business, the fear of flying can really become debilitating. It can lead to avoidance; or it can lead to all kinds of what we call compensatory phenomenon. For example, I tell myself that I can drive to my destination faster than I can fly. I have to check into the airport—you know how long that can take?! Then I have to drive there and park; then I have to rent a car....

I have experienced fear of flying, myself. The last time I flew to Fresno it was on American Eagle, which has propellers. The aisles are very small. American Eagle looked fine to me, until I got on board and found out that the people putting my luggage on board were the same people who were flying the plane, and they were both very young. I prefer that pilots have a little bit of gray hair. I noticed that these pilots were about twenty-five years of age, and that just didn't match my perception of what a pilot is to look like. I had difficulty with this, and since that time, I have driven to Fresno.

Let's say I had to get to Fresno for a trial as an expert witness; I would start two days earlier and do some deep breathing exercises. I'd try to work myself up to breathing in for seven to eight seconds and breathing out for twelve to thirteen seconds so that I would breath in more than I would breath out. With lots of practice and closing my eyes, I'd probably do this all the way to Fresno. That is one way to overcome the fear of flying.

FEAR OF FLYING

Fear 101

There are many types of fear. Behavioral patterns differ among individuals according to his or her association to fear. Some clinicians have suggested that we are born with two fears—the fear of loud noises and the fear of falling. All the rest are learned fears.

When examined, it seems absurd that we would teach ourselves to be afraid. We do not make a concerted effort to become frightened of things. Often it is a subconscious occurrence. We are introduced to a certain situation, and our mental and physical stimuli suggest danger, which triggers the fear. We now have an unpleasant frame of reference with the situation or thing that caused the fear. Each time we are confronted with the experience, we become frightened.

Fears People Have

Based upon a survey conducted, individuals revealed issues that caused them fear.

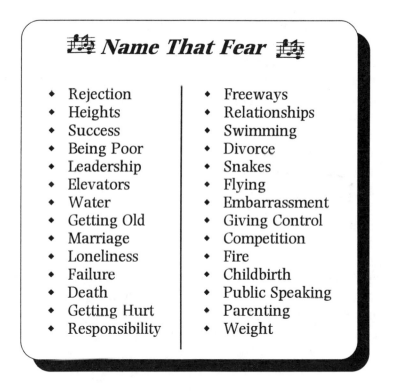

Name That Fear

- Rejection
- Heights
- Success
- Being Poor
- Leadership
- Elevators
- Water
- Getting Old
- Marriage
- Loneliness
- Failure
- Death
- Getting Hurt
- Responsibility

- Freeways
- Relationships
- Swimming
- Divorce
- Snakes
- Flying
- Embarrassment
- Giving Control
- Competition
- Fire
- Childbirth
- Public Speaking
- Parenting
- Weight

In our current example, we see how fear impacts a child, and how the child's fears can be worked through with the assistance of his parents. The following example demonstrates a different type of fear; one where clinical help is needed—an adult responding to the fear of getting emotionally hurt—resulting in the fear of intimate and close interpersonal relationships.

Overcoming Doubt, Fear and Procrastination

Interpersonal Relationships—The Fear Of Getting Hurt.

It is a gorgeous day. The sun is shinning and palm trees are gently swaying in the morning breeze. Below my hotel room, I can hear young children laughing and splashing about as they play in the pool. In the distance is a beautifully landscaped golf course with acres and acres of majestic trees. Off to the right, I can see a thin line of cars traversing, taking its occupants to and from their daily responsibilities. As I continue to survey the morning, I notice a couple basking in the therapeutic warmth of the Jacuzzi. For a moment, I find myself fixated on the female; almost as if I hope to gain some insight into myself through careful examination of her behavior. It's funny, as I watch her interact with whom I assume to be her husband, I instinctively know how she will respond as another female approaches.

I think she is going to move closer to her husband and put her arms about him, or display some loving gesture to put the other woman on notice that "this one" is taken! Like a director calling out action on the set of a well-scripted movie, her every move is calculated, as she makes a swan-like movement toward her husband, stroking his chest and placing her arms around his neck as she ever so lovingly rests her head gently on his shoulder.

Recounting her behavior, I think no one could possibly be that frightened and insecure. Then I remember the real reason I am here in this hotel room alone. Philip and I have been estranged for two months now. It feels like two decades. I miss him so much. He said we needed space. He was feeling smothered, and he couldn't deal with my fear of losing him to every woman that came within five feet. He could no longer tolerate my intense insecurities regarding his being faithful to me.

He was sick and tired of repeating how much he loved me, and that he had no intention of leaving me for another woman.

I remember the last thing Philip said before he left, "I love you Christine, and you just don't seem to believe me. No matter how hard I try, or what I do, you consistently push me further and further away from you. You're too preoccupied with your fear of getting hurt and being abandoned. I have bent over backwards to understand how you must feel after your relationship with your first husband. You keep embracing these insecure feelings that I will abandon you for another woman. Christine, it's just gotten out of hand. Your behavior is not normal; you really need to seek professional help."

After Philip and I separated, I was devastated. I took a leave of absence from my job to sort things out. Philip keeps in touch with me; he's always been a very compassionate and considerate person. He doesn't make any promises that he can't keep; however, he does let me know that he cares. He knows that I am in therapy; he even said that he could see the progress.

It's true, I have made a great deal of progress; however, I still have a long way to go. It's funny, that doesn't seem to bother me. As a matter of fact, I look forward to it. In looking back, I must admit that I don't see how Philip tolerated my behavior as long as he did.

I don't know whether Philip is dating or not; he never talks about it. I am certainly not dating, I don't think I'm emotionally stable to take the plunge. Deep inside, I am hoping that as I continue to make progress, Philip and I can have the kind of relationship that he so richly deserves. He is a good man.

I met Philip on a flight to Spain. I was the stylist on a photo shoot for an ad campaign for Hosch, Inc.

Philip was on vacation. I couldn't believe a man this handsome would be vacationing alone. He gave new meaning to the expression *tall, dark and handsome!* I remember how good he smelled as he took his seat next to me. He was so polite; he even offered to give up his window seat. I thought to myself, "What a gentleman; they don't make them like that anymore." For the first half hour we flew in silence. I was positive he was married.

Then from out of the blue he asked, "Do you live in Spain, or are you just vacationing?" I was so stunned, I could hardly respond. I took a moment—a *brief* moment—to regain my composure before answering. I said, "No. I am here on business." For some strange reason, my answer seemed to really spark his interest. From then on, it was non-stop conversation. It was refreshing to meet a man so easy to talk with. We talked about everything: sports, politics, and fashions. This was a new one for me; most men don't engage in conversations regarding fashion. But Philip seemed to enjoy it.

It was funny. I was so nervous trying to make a good impression on this man, I couldn't even eat. It was reminiscent of some love-sick high school teenager out on her first date. I thought, "This is pathetic. A woman in her forties should certainly have herself pulled together better than this!"

My assignment lasted two weeks, and I saw Philip every evening. We would have dinner and discuss how coincidental it was that our lives had so much in common. I had worked to help put Sebastian, my first husband, through medical school. The year after he graduated, Sebastian left me for Dominique, *the other woman.* He had met her one summer at Lakeview Hospital where he worked as an intern.

In a sense, Philip's situation was similar in that we both had failed marriages. During Philip's marriage he worked and attended law school which left him very little time for anything else. As a result, he and his wife Jennifer grew further and further apart. The relationship finally ended in divorce.

Philip seems to have healed. However, now that I am in therapy, I've come to understand that I have never quite gotten over Sebastian leaving me for another woman, especially after the sacrifice I made to put him through medical school—I even put my own career on hold.

Identifying the Problem

Christine's situation is very common. She failed to fully identify the problem and put closure on the incident in her former marriage to Sebastian. She believed that her husband's betrayal was indicative of the way she would be treated by every man. Therefore, she would have to insure that this would not happen to her again. She felt that by building in safety measures this would give her the added reassurance she needed.

The first step is to recognize that you have a problem. In Christine's case, she didn't realize the severity of her behavior until Philip left her. She was afraid of getting hurt and being abandoned in a relationship. The fear of loneliness and rejection only added fuel to the fire. Her fears increased her anxiety level which resulted in her becoming insecure in a close, loving relationship. She acted out her insecurity by becoming suspicious of her mate and not trusting him.

Her philosophy was to be on the defense and look for premature signs of infidelity: Test your mates level of commitment. And above all, never trust another woman—she only wants to steal your mate. In order to protect what is *yours*, you must stake your claim and let the other woman know that this is your property—and he is off limits.

Her fears and insecurities caused her to put men on the defense to prove their affections and loyalty to her. Her overpowering need for reassurance was emotionally draining and too much for any man to bear. Christine drove men away and Philip was not the first, but he was the only one who cared enough to tell her the truth.

In therapy, Christine learned how to evaluate her fears. She learned to understand that Sebastian had a great deal of responsibility for their marriage failing. His choice to leave her for another woman was not a sign that *all* men behaved in this manner. In retrospect, Christine was able to see that Sebastian was insecure and had problems of his own.

Using role reversal, the therapist was able to demonstrate the overwhelming burden she placed on Philip by being so suspicious, insecure and needy. She was able to see that this type of behavior was emotionally damaging to their relationship. She treated Philip like a prisoner trying to isolate him from other women in order to protect her position, not to mention her constantly putting Philip on the defense by making him jump through hoops to prove his love and devotion.

One of the most important revelations occurred when Christine was able to dispel the belief that she was not qualified to hold a man on her own merit. She was an attractive woman, very bright, with a witty sense of humor; that's what attracted men to her. She began to affirm those attributes within her own mind. This gave her an additional sense of security. She learned that a man could appreciate her for who she is, and there was no reason for her to feel threatened by another woman.

Healthy or Unhealthy?

"When are doubt, fear and procrastination un-healthy? At what point should you seek professional help? Doubt, fear and procrastination are all normal responses to environmental stimuli and life stressors. The first step is to recognize that they are normal reactions. The point in time when someone needs to seek professional advice is when one of the three have become incapacitating. When a person cannot do something because of doubt, fear and procrastination, that's when some kind of help needs to be sought," stated Dr. Cecil Whiting.

In an interview with psychologist, Dr. Jane Myers Drew, I asked: "How do you distinguish between healthy and unhealthy fear?" She answered, "You distinguish one from the other by how often you feel afraid, and how severe it is. If I am doing a radio show and a half hour before it begins, I feel a little tense, that's okay. My fear gets me to bustle around, look through my notes, and get everything just right. If I am afraid for days (it doesn't happen any longer) and I get depressed, then I think it is time to go see a therapist, and do something about it. I don't think we can work it (excessive fear) out by ourselves. We human beings aren't meant to be on our own, and so often this idea of success is sort of the American way of thinking—I pull myself up by my bootstraps—I do it. I think uniting together and helping one another is where our real strength lies."

3) Doubt And Its Relationship To Fear

Doubt is the child of poor preparation and poor research. Knowledge breeds confidence in my experience; and the more confident I am regarding a particular task, the less doubtful I become.
— *S. Barry Hamdani*

Doubt takes on many attributes, from disbelief in one's ability to succeed or accomplish a goal, to causing fear of failure. A noted clinician defined doubt as fear without the physiological reaction. For some, doubt is believing what others feel you are not capable of. Doubt can make you feel inadequate, causing you to feel that you are not qualified, skilled, knowledgeable, or smart enough. Once this takes place, you are sure that success is out of your reach.

Doubt Can Be Traced Back To Your Childhood.

The roots of self-doubt can often be traced back to one's childhood. The parent's negative reaction on a consistent basis to a child's performance, builds the foundation of doubt. The child sees his efforts as fruitless, and feels that no matter how hard he tries, or what he does, no good will come of his efforts. He begins to see himself as worthless.

Doubt and Its Relationship to Fear

So often, parents are blind to the damage they inflict on their child's self-esteem. Some parents place stringent expectations on their child. What seems very natural and simplistic to the parent, becomes overwhelming for the child who has little or no real life experience. A child may not know how to reason or think through *all* the necessary steps to accomplish a task, especially in the face of adversity.

In most cases, the child has been ridiculed and shamed for his efforts, so much so that now he is afraid to ask for help; consequently, he continues to repeat the same scenario. The parent must have patience and understanding in order to effectively communicate.

It is important for the parents to see the situation through their child's eyes, and realize the enormous weight that the duties, tasks and responsibilities have on the youngster. The parents must not become annoyed when they have to repeat simple instructions. They should reward accomplishments for those efforts completed successfully, and encourage the child to continue to try to accomplish those tasks for which he has failed. The process should be one of gently reassuring him that it is all right that he did not completely understand how to do the duties the first time; and letting him know that they are happy to go over the instructions again until he can successfully accomplish the goal. This process builds confidence in the child, and lets him know that he is okay, even if he tried and did not succeed initially. The child also feels a level of comfort in coming to the parents and asking for help, or just saying, "I don't understand, can you tell me, again?"

This type of interaction builds a secure, healthy child who will not doubt himself when it comes to responsibility. He knows that it is all right to fail and try again; and it is okay to ask for help when he needs it. It lets him know that his value as a person has not diminished as a result of the experience. The child's self-worth remains intact even though he does not comprehend a given task at the onset. The child acquires an understanding that no one is perfect and to err is human.

Another harmful way parents create doubt is through competition. Some parents compare one child to the other. They may suggest that one child does something better than the other. Children are always vying for the approval and acceptance of their parents. This places the children in a competitive situation where they may fail and be ridiculed for not living up to the performance of another, thus creating doubt in the children and instituting the age-old problem of sibling rivalry.

As a result, children fear that they may lose their position with their parents, if they do not live up to the standards placed before them. They are conditioned to doubt that they will succeed, and they fear that they will let their parents down. Constantly trying to meet the performance or out-do the performance of another places far too much stress on children. This conditioning makes them feel guilty and inadequate.

Parents act out these messages in many ways: "Why can't you be like your brother? He always gets good grades! I wish you were as smart as your friends!" Translated to the level of children's comprehension, here's what they hear: "Something must be wrong with you; you aren't as smart as your brother! You are dumb and inferior to your friends." These negative messages create doubt in children, and the doubt creates fear. They doubt whether they will ever live up to the expectations of their parents.

Doubt and Its Relationship to Fear

Children who are exposed to this type of behavior often carry their feelings of doubt into their adult lives. Doubt is acted out in their work relationships, and in other interpersonal encounters. As adults, perhaps the players have changed somewhat; instead of their parents, it may be a boss or spouse whose approval and acceptance they seek, but the story remains the same: Fear of not being able to compete with others or not being able to meet with the approval of others continues to hamper their success.

The overwhelming feelings of doubt and fear give procrastinators the license to continue to do so. In short, success is jeopardized as a result of doubt. Claiming failure before one tries makes it easy to avoid stepping up to the plate and risking the false sense of security procrastinators receive by putting things off, or simply doing nothing at all.

With doubt and fear present, procrastination is imminent. The procrastinator feels no matter what he does, he will be viewed as a failure, and ultimately lose his position in the relationship. So why bother? Believing that to be true, he will enjoy the sanctity of withdrawing his efforts completely.

Is There a Relationship Between Doubt and Fear?

Dr. Whiting sees a direct correlation between doubt and fear. "Fear engenders doubt. If you're a student who has had all the preparation you can have and cannot make the next move, at a certain point you begin to doubt (it's personalized doubt). You doubt your ability to do what you have been trained to do, or thought you could do.

"Doubt and fear run together. Doubt is the inability to move, primarily because of fear. You fear that performance will be inadequate. I don't want to limit it to performance—the fear of lack of safety can be a factor. Along with doubt and fear, the final stage is procrastination: _Stay away from it. Avoid it; don't do it. Put it off. Maybe next week._ This is the flow of what happens to people in terms of their circumstances."

Doubt—The Human Experience

Dr. Jane Myers Drew knew doubt on a very personal level: "Doubt seems to have more to do with myself. Am I good enough? That is the one that's the hardest for me. From childhood on, that's the one I had to deal with. My family was rather shame-based: _What's wrong with you? I told you not to do that!_ That's something I've had to work with and really battle a lot.

"I overcame doubt by taking small steps, even with the fear of going ahead to the next level and seeing how I did. By having good friends, I could see reflected in their caring that I was okay the way I was. Their attitude was that if I should fail, they loved me, anyway. I could make mistakes and have failures; to be human is to have failures. I worry about people who think they should be successful and _on_ the whole time."

Worry—Are You A Victim?

Product of Worry   **_Results of Confidence_**

Many successful people worry; however, they do not see themselves as victims of worry. In interviewing successful individuals and their philosophies regarding worry, here are some thought-provoking comments I received when I posed the question, _"Are you a victim of worry?"_

Gail Blake-Smith, consultant and human resources manager for Pacific Bell: "I am no longer a victim of worry, due to my strong belief system. I recognize that worrying is nothing but wasted energy; things will work out. The more faith and belief you have in the Lord and His word, the less anxiety or worry you will have.

"It is human to allow some anxiety or worry to come into your mind, but how you react to it is predicated upon your belief system. In my opinion, I think that attitude is the whole thing, and when I find myself entering into a cynical mode of worry, having doubt or fear, then I go back to my source of belief—Jesus Christ."

Roberta Pierce, vice-president of sales and operations for VIP Employment Services: "I have been a victim of worry. I am not a victim of worry any longer. I overcame this by recognizing that it isn't healthy to worry. There is no sense in being worried about something over which you have no control. Being concerned is one thing, but worrying is a whole different subject. I realize that it's okay to be concerned; but there's no use in worrying, because worrying isn't going to change the outcome of anything. I can be concerned maybe, because being concerned might give me some direction. Worry is just useless and futile."

S. Barry Hamdani, one of Atlanta's most successful entrepreneurs: "I am a victim of sporadic worry. Once I find myself in the process of worrying, I ask

49

myself whether I have done all I can do to bring about the desired outcome; if not, I must act immediately. If I do not act, I will worry. If I fail to make a decision, I worry."

Carlease Burke, a successful actress and comedienne: She recently appeared with John Travolta in the film, *Get Shorty*, and has found her cure-all for worry. "I realize there are things that are out of my control, and things that I can't do anything about...it's just a waste of time and energy to fret or worry about them. Worry takes time away from doing more constructive things. It positions me in the *negative* all the time, because worry is a negative thing. How can I see the solution if I am worrying and fretting? I've learned to release things that I have no control over."

Gail Taylor Walton, program coordinator of physicians training at King-Drew Medical Center: "No, I can't say that I am a victim of worry. I feel that when you worry you're executing yourself twice. To worry beforehand is putting the torture before the real torture. I worry about things that have already started happening. I generally don't worry about things that could happen."

Dr. Jane Myers Drew, PhD, psychologist in private practice in Newport Beach, California: "Worry is putting energy into something you can't do anything about. It's sort of a compulsive behavior that doesn't have any rewards, and it doesn't move you forward. It keeps you in that squirrel cage going round and round.

"There are three things I might do to prevent worry. The first thing is: I might sit down and start journalizing. I write my own feelings down to evaluate what's going on. Secondly, I might call a close friend and say, 'There's something going on. I need to talk. I need to talk this situation through with you to see if I can get a better perspective than what I have right now, and to see what is actually going on.' Lastly, if there isn't anything I can do about it, I might do something pleasurable to take my mind off the problem."

Self-Confidence

It becomes extremely difficult to stay positive in the throes of self-doubt. We are born with a clean slate, and life experiences are added as we grow, some more positive than others. Unfortunately, as children we have very little frame of reference on how to disseminate unnecessary emotional baggage. As a result, these painful, negative experiences are registered on our slate with an emotional sticky-note that reads: *This was not a positive experience, so something must be wrong with me!*

As we mature and confront similar situations, we reflect back to our mental rolodex and up pops that sticky-note to remind us that we have problems functioning in this arena. We read it, absorb it and place an emotional roadblock in our path known as doubt. Once doubt is comfortably in place, its old friend, fear, rushes in to reinforce the fact that we are no good at this, so we better leave well enough alone.

Part of doubt stems from low self-esteem and one's lack of self-confidence. You question your ability to succeed, and you feel that you aren't qualified to complete a task or a project; this ultimately prevents you from going forward. Lack of self-confidence is a major cause of procrastination. If you know that there is a chance you may risk getting hurt or jeopardizing your social position, you immediately ask yourself, "Why should I place myself in that position?"

In order to move past these feelings, you need to tap into what makes you feel good about yourself and your ability to succeed. Along the road to maturation, on your slate, you have stacked up some positive experiences as well (some good sticky-notes)—some wins. These are the experiences that you shall call on to reinforce your self-worth.

Remembering how good it felt to accomplish a goal and the fact that you did it, are the feelings you want to conjure up. You want to reflect on the emotional stimuli that got you from point A to point B. Taking that same energy and positive thinking, you will infuse that same attitude into a project that you have considerable doubt regarding your ability to succeed.

Elevating Your Self-Confidence

One very good way to elevate your self-esteem and self-confidence is through reflecting on positive experiences. What victories have you experienced in your life? What have been your most significant accomplishments? Use these experiences to feel good about yourself and what *you* can accomplish.

In looking back, you may recall that you probably had some concerns at the onset regarding those victories. However, you succeeded in spite of the obstacles. You are no different from anyone else. Successful people aren't exempt from doubt, fear and procrastination, they just respond differently.

As a business consultant, the majority of my clients did not hire me because they were deficient in their business acumen; they hired me because they were stuck in some emotional holding pattern as a result of something negative someone had said to them. They began to question whether or not they were making sound decisions with respect to going into business, and for some, even being in business at all.

More often than not, the culprit would be someone close to them; someone holding an emotional tie whose opinion they valued, and whose acceptance and approval they desired, such as a spouse, significant other, mother, etc.

I recall one client in particular. She was held hostage emotionally by her husband, her mother and her three brothers. They were all telling her how crazy she was, and how insane it was for her to even entertain the thought of going into business. Not only did she go to the valley of self-doubt, she had camped out and set up permanent residence!

I began to counsel with her, and the first thing I had her do was to make a list of all the reasons why she felt going into business was good for her. Next, we took a look at her knowledge and expertise in the field (she was more than qualified).

Before moving on to something that may have some negative consequence, such as listing the cons regarding going into business, I asked her to make a victory list, a list of all the major accomplishments that she had experienced in her life. I encouraged her to reflect on how good she felt after her victories. Then I asked her to examine some of the concerns she had prior to challenging these projects, and what methods she utilized to overcome her concerns, thus allowing her to move forward to victory.

Prior to her next visit, I copied her two positive lists in large-bold type, as a constant reminder of her victories and all the good reasons why this business was right for her. During the consultation, I keep them right before her. This was going to be significantly important, since we had to deal with some negative issues regarding her family's opinions of her and her ability to go into business.

We took a sheet of paper and listed each family member and his or her objections. We examined them one by one. Each time I would see her seriously considering the possibility that they might be right, I would steer her back to her two positive lists. You could see the change in her facial expression as she was reminded of the greatness within her.

We named one list *Yes, I Can*, and the other, *My Personal Victories*. She had them laminated and keeps them in her office; each time she faces adversity she turns to her lists. She says that when she sees them she thinks to herself, "Yes I can, because I have had problems before and achieved success in spite of the obstacles—I remained victorious!"

Just the mere reminder of your successes and the greatness within you, will help elevate you from self-doubt and lack of self-confidence. Try it; it works!

Mr. Hamdani, a very successful entrepreneur in Atlanta, knows how to counteract doubt through building self-confidence. "I feel best upon the completion of a task well done. I feel that way because this is the most present victory. I must draw upon that victory whenever I am feeling down. I must use its memory to chase away fear, doubt and procrastination which await me in the future. It is the fuel which will propel my dreams in the future. It is the manifestation of what I can do in the present."

4) *Procrastination—I Have Tomorrow!*

Tomorrow has its own agenda. Procrastination has no right to infringe its duties and responsibilities on tomorrow.

Are You a Procrastinator?

The buzz words for procrastinators are *putting things off.* Procrastinators have a list of handy clichés that work for them. Perhaps you have even used one or two yourself. Do you recognize these two? *Better late than never. There's always tomorrow.* Procrastinators are notorious for certain behavioral patterns.

In conducting a survey of some of the world's greatest procrastinators, we developed a list of the most common things they do. It's called, *You Might Be A Procrastinator If...* Review the list on page 56; check the appropriate boxes to see if you identify character traits that fit your personality. If any of the excuses fit, then you are a prime candidate for the procrastinator's oath on page 57.

Creatures of Habit

It has been said that we are *creatures of habit.* Our habits often take us into emotional realms that are very uncomfortable. Once there, we struggle to free ourselves from the turmoil. After achieving freedom, we vow never to repeat the same scenario. Needless to say, some habits are certainly not positive, and procrastination ranks high on the list.

You Might Be A Procrastinator If...

☐ You are always fashionably late.
☐ You do your Christmas shopping on the 24th.
☐ You're pregnant and you put off packing your suitcase until your water breaks.
☐ The clothes hamper is full and you say it is half empty.
☐ You plan to mow the lawn, but watch football instead.
☐ You get an extension on your taxes and receive a penalty for missing the new deadline.
☐ You make a New Year's Resolution and fail to keep it.
☐ You have a daily planner and never follow it.
☐ More than 20% of your to-do list appears on next year's calendar.
☐ You plan to open a new business and don't because you fear failure.
☐ You are assigned a project and you wait until the eleventh hour to complete it.
☐ You deny doing what you know is right.
☐ You have no respect for time.
☐ You don't plan, organize and structure events or projects.
☐ You think you have tomorrow.
☐ It takes guilt to motivate you.
☐ You allow fear to overpower you.
☐ You doubt your ability to complete your goal.
☐ You allow others to take control of your life.
☐ You believe that success is out of your reach.
☐ Failure brings you more comfort than success.
☐ You have an exam and wait until the night before to study.
☐ Your initial thought is doubt.
☐ You set appointments and never keep them.
☐ You reach into the closet and find nothing to wear.
☐ You don't retrieve phone messages within 24 hours.
☐ You make excuses for not getting to the gym.
☐ You find yourself avoiding responsibility.
☐ Lying feels better than telling the truth.
☐ You waste productive time.
☐ You always retreat to your comfort zone.
☐ Doing everything at the last minute has become a way of life.
☐ Each year you promise to stop smoking.

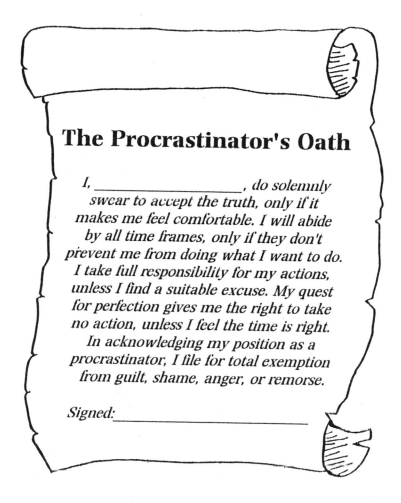

The Procrastinator's Oath

I, _____, do solemnly swear to accept the truth, only if it makes me feel comfortable. I will abide by all time frames, only if they don't prevent me from doing what I want to do. I take full responsibility for my actions, unless I find a suitable excuse. My quest for perfection gives me the right to take no action, unless I feel the time is right. In acknowledging my position as a procrastinator, I file for total exemption from guilt, shame, anger, or remorse.

Signed: _____

One would think that having experience with these issues would be enough to prevent constant repetition of behavioral patterns that culminate in negative emotional experiences. If the latter be true, why is it that we—time and time again—place ourselves in these emotionally uncomfortable situations born out of the bosom of procrastination? Each of us has the sole responsibility to examine our behavior and expose the real reasons we procrastinate.

Procrastination has an enemy—guilt! When referring to the term guilt, you probably view the emotion as negative. Among the list of emotional experiences, guilt does not lend itself to making you feel very good about yourself. Feeling guilty is a true drain on your positive spirit. It is a very uncomfortable emotion.

Guilt is a nagging emotion brought on by your conscience. The conscious mind constantly reminds you of what you are doing wrong. It is like a dripping faucet. Each drip irritates you more than the last, until finally you are driven to right the wrong. The harder you try to turn your conscience off, or stop thinking of the issue causing you to feel guilty, the more irritating it becomes each and every time you continue to think about it.

Can feeling guilty really help or deter one from procrastination? This annoyance caused by your conscience is the motivating factor that guilt creates. The annoyance itself is what motivates us to do something to eliminate the guilt, thus preventing the desire to procrastinate. In essence, guilt can be the motivating factor for action or change. In this sense we can look at guilt in a positive way. The emotional feelings caused by guilt have twin-fold benefits: guilt can prevent us from procrastinating. Once in the throes of procrastination, guilt can motivate us to cease the behavior. With respect to procrastination, guilt does have its benefits. The following scenario demonstrates how guilt acts as a motivating factor to stop procrastination.

Guilt—The Motivating Factor

Demitrius Snowden was a law student at a prestigious university as well as a brilliant and witty comedian. He appeared regularly at comedy clubs—much to the delight of his friends. Demitrius had a special gift; he could compose material for his one-man comedy routine without the least bit of effort. Fellow comics admired his gift and consistently commissioned Demitrius to write comedy routines for their showcase.

During summer and spring break, he would perform at various comedy clubs to standing-room only crowds. Instantly, in his first season of performing, he received second billing to some of the better known comics in the area. During his third season, he was one of the most sought-after comedians. He always received top billing.

Encouraged by his peers to pursue a career as a comedian, he found it very difficult to ignore the advice of his friends. Making this decision meant that he would have to drop out of law school. As Demitrius contemplated pursuing his dream full time, he thought to himself, "Being on stage and the center of attention gives me such a rush. All my life, I have wanted to be popular in my own right, and being a comedian fulfills that desire." Making this decision found Demitrius struggling with procrastination.

His parents were well educated and had invested a great deal of time and effort to impress upon him the value of getting a good education. In college Demitrius was blessed with the ability to grasp concepts and retain information. He could read a book in nothing flat, and maintain full retention. His peers marveled at his ability to wait until the last minute to study for a test, and still receive one of the highest grades in the class.

However, there was another side to his personality. Spawned by his popularity as a comedian, Demitrius became a *party animal.* He was very handsome and well liked by everyone, not to mention being an excellent dancer. His name was at the top of every party list. He loved to have a good time. Unfortunately, he would have a good time at the expense of doing important things.

Demitrius had a second weakness. He longed to please people. He found it extremely difficult to say no to his friends and those whom he loved. Pleasing people and making them happy was the main reason he chose to become a comedian.

With less than a year-and-a half left to complete his law degree, Demitrius announced that he wanted to drop out of law school to become a stand-up comic. His parents were livid; this was a disgrace. They had groomed Demitrius to become an attorney and to take his place alongside his father in the law firm. No one in the family labored in the arts.

Monica, his older sister, was in her last year of medical school. After completion she was slated to open her own private practice, specializing in sports medicine. His mother was a professor at a leading university; and his father was an attorney at a prestigious law firm whose title had five or six surnames gilded on the office door—touting the names of all the partners, including Demitrius' father.

Although both his parents came from humble beginnings, they were able to provide a better life for their children through hard work, education and excellent investment opportunities. They had saved money to launch Monica's medical practice, and had carved a niche for Demitrius in his father's law firm, with the intent of Demitrius ultimately joining ranks as a full partner. To his parents, it was a plan etched in stone with no room for deviation.

As a result of his overnight success as a comedian, Demitrius' rational judgment had become clouded when it came to his career goals. He had made a solemn promise to himself and to his parents to finish law school and become a partner in his father's law firm. Although being a comedian is an acceptable profession, his parents maintained that he still needed a college education behind him.

In an effort to appease his parents, Demitrius agreed to finish law school; however, he would do so later, after securing his career as a comedian. In trying to rationalize with their impetuous son, they struck a nerve in the core of his being. His mother argued that consenting to finish college later was nothing more than procrastination. His willingness to put off his education now for future completion was a dangerous move, and he would live to regret it.

Desperate to get her son to see her point, his mother pleaded, "Why put off tomorrow what you can do today? All your adult life you have waited until the last minute and consistently put things off. You can't keep this up; you aren't going to always be so lucky!" He acknowledged her point, but held firm to his decision to complete college after he had put a few years into his craft as a comic.

During summer break, his conscience played havoc with his head. His sense of guilt made him miserable, mainly because he had disappointed his parents and disrupted his career goals. During that very difficult time, all he could focus on was how guilty he felt for even considering dropping out of college.

At the close of the summer, he decided to put closure on the guilt that had destroyed his entire summer. In an open letter to his parents he wrote:

....much credit must be given to both you and Dad for raising me with a sense of responsibility. Throughout the entire summer, I have thought about what you have said about college. You have raised me to make good decisions, and I know that is why my conscience has caused me such pain. I have been racked with guilt, and what's worse is the joy I once found as a comic has gone. If nothing else but to stop these feelings of guilt, I have decided to return to college this fall and pursue my stand-up routine part-time.

For Demitrius, guilt was a motivating factor. He went on to complete law school and passed the bar. He worked in his father's law firm and became a full partner. The experience was the beginning of a learning process; Demitrius learned to use guilt as a motivating factor to avoid procrastination.

The Origin of Guilt

Our behavior plays a large part in our feelings of guilt. We feel guilty when we do something wrong. So it is safe to say that wrongdoing and guilt usually go hand-in-hand. In the wake of the *wrongdoing,* we find that there is punishment or some consequence to pay—be it real or imagined.

When we commit an act that we know is wrong, we blame our actions for how bad we are feeling. These bad feelings manifest themselves in many ways. We may feel that we were stupid for doing what we did. Some individuals feel shamed by their actions, while others may feel a sense of worthlessness brought on by an overwhelming sense of guilt. Is our behavior the only cause of guilt? Can our mere thoughts make us feel guilty?

The conscious mind plays an active role in feelings of guilt. We are brought up to respect certain principles of social conduct and thought. While we may not commit an act of wrongdoing, the fact that we entertained the thought makes us feel guilty. Thank goodness we have a conscience that acts as a weigh station between right and wrong. Otherwise, we would be out of control!

The following example further demonstrates how our innermost thoughts of wrongdoing can make us feel guilty, even though we may not initiate the act.

Feeling Guilty as a Result of Your Thoughts

Theresa Pedigrew attended a fairly upscale high school and socialized with girls whose parents were in the more affluent income bracket. During the spring, a new family moved into the neighborhood. Theresa's mother, Mrs. Pedigrew, thought of herself as the official chairman of the welcoming committee. She felt it was her civic duty to go over and welcome them to the neighborhood.

During her visit, she discovered that the new neighbors also had a daughter the same age as Theresa. Her name was Beatrice and she would be attending Ridgemont High, the same high school as Theresa. Knowing this, that evening Mrs. Pedigrew arranged for Beatrice and Theresa to meet, so that Theresa could introduce Beatrice to her friends, and help her to get acquainted with her new school.

Beatrice was an attractive young lady, quiet and shy, and very religious. Theresa, on the other hand, was

63

more of a social butterfly and felt uneasy around Beatrice. Because Theresa's mother had suggested that she look after Beatrice and show her around, she felt obligated to do so. Theresa told Beatrice to meet her in the cafeteria the next morning before the first bell.

The next day Theresa and her friends were assembled in the cafeteria when she spotted Beatrice. She signaled for Beatrice to come and join her and her friends at the table. She greeted Beatrice and introduced her to her peers. As Beatrice took a seat, Theresa noticed that she had a Bible. One of Theresa's friends turned to her and whispered, "Where did you get this *Bible Toting Christian*?" Although Beatrice didn't hear the comment, it embarrassed Theresa, greatly.

The atmosphere at the table became so quiet you could hear a pin drop. Slowly, one-by-one, the other girls began to make excuses and leave the table, until only Theresa and Beatrice remained.

Theresa did keep her word; she showed Beatrice to her first class. Before she could leave, Beatrice asked, "Where shall I meet you for lunch?" Remembering the reaction of her peers, Theresa wanted to tell her, "Don't bother!" Reluctantly she replied, "Meet me in the cafeteria."

All morning during class, Theresa found it difficult to concentrate. Her thoughts were of Beatrice. She kept thinking how square and homely Beatrice was, and that she felt ashamed to have her around her friends. Theresa felt guilty, not of her actions, but of her thoughts. She felt guilty for having these negative thoughts regarding Beatrice. After all, Beatrice was a very nice young lady. It wasn't her fault that she didn't fit in. Theresa knew that these feelings were wrong.

Theresa's self-esteem and self-confidence began to suffer. Her fear of losing her social status within the group was the chief cause. She felt her friends were making a mockery of her relationship with Beatrice. She was afraid that her friends would not approve of Beatrice. She doubted whether they would continue to embrace her as part of the group if she maintained a relationship with Beatrice. Theresa had to deal with the issue of acceptance from her peers. *The Acceptance Principle* is explored in more detail in chapter five.

For Theresa to take a stand and maintain a relationship with Beatrice required deep introspection and soul-searching. She had to ask herself how important it was to gain the approval and acceptance of her friends in order to have a relationship with someone else. Did she *really* want to be held to those strict standards of control by her peers? Or, would she stand for what she believed in, even if it meant alienating herself from the group?

Her conscience got the better of her; she took a stand and decided to maintain her relationship with Beatrice. For the first few days they ate lunch by themselves, and walked to class by themselves. All of a sudden a miracle took place; one after the other, Theresa's friends began to come around.

In the two scenarios illustrating guilt, we see the results of guilt in both action and thought. In the case of Demitrius Snowden, guilt was the motivating factor which helped him eliminate his tendency to procrastinate regarding his future. In this instance, we see guilt in a positive vein, giving rise to the fact that guilt can serve as a motivating factor to prevent us from procrastinating.

Guilt manifests itself through behavior—our actions—and through the conscious mind—our thoughts. Theresa's experience demonstrates the enormous power guilt has on our thought process. If guilt is associated with preventing individuals from wrong doing or thinking wrong, in order to find peace, they must *right* the wrong.

Guilt can also have a negative side. It is counter-productive when it erodes self-esteem and self-confidence. "The older I get, the more I see how guilt can be useless," stated Dr. Jane Myers Drew. "A part of me is making another part feel guilty for doing what I don't want to do. I try to get more in touch with what I really want to do.

"When we are younger, we are still operating off of what Mom and Dad told us. There's a part of us that doesn't want to do something, and another part that says that we should, and so we feel guilty. There are so many choices out here, I don't have to do most anything—really. I do need to make a living so I can keep the body and soul together. However, I don't have to do it in any particular way. I have all sorts of choices.

"Part of me would like to be famous and make great contributions to the world, and another part of me is saying (the wiser part) as I am going along my path—and writing my books—if that happens that is fine. And if it doesn't, then that's okay, too. I don't have to be driven to get that. If it happens and if that's my path, I am going to take steps, but I don't have to make it happen. There was a part of me, not too long ago that said, 'I am going to make it happen!' I let go of that, and I am much happier."

Denial—Where Are My Excuses?

In chapter one, *Accepting the Truth*, armed with a number of excuses, Frank had a negative disposition toward accepting the truth. He found great comfort in rejecting the truth by adopting a series of useless excuses, better known as denial. Frank's philosophy mandated that when he felt guilty about how he was feeling, or what someone said or thought about him, he could always retreat to his comfort zone and select the excuse that suited his fancy.

Frank is not exempt when it comes to operating in the denial mode; many people find themselves practicing this philosophy. It allows them to ease their conscience while they continue to go about their business

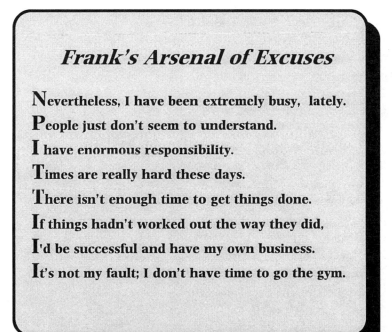

Frank's Arsenal of Excuses

Nevertheless, I have been extremely busy, lately.

People just don't seem to understand.

I have enormous responsibility.

Times are really hard these days.

There isn't enough time to get things done.

If things hadn't worked out the way they did,

I'd be successful and have my own business.

It's not my fault; I don't have time to go the gym.

practicing the art of procrastination. What excuses do you use to justify procrastinating? Dr. Whiting summed it up appropriately when he stated, "Denial is when you lie to yourself and you don't know that you are lying."

Denial Promulgates Procrastination

Does denial really make you feel better about your tendency to procrastinate? Denial is the fuel to the fire that ignites the behavioral pattern known to many as procrastination. It is your license to pick excuse mechanisms that will buy you time to procrastinate, and will temporarily make you feel good while doing so. Denial does not eradicate the problems associated with procrastination, it only buys you time to continue operating in that mode.

Leaving the Comfort Zone

We all have a safe haven, or a place inside of us with a voice that tells us everything is okay. We set boundaries or parameters on how close people can get to us. We know instinctively just what activities we can do with little or no effort. We have rituals which we perform in our daily lives that make us feel secure. We reserve parts of our lives from others in order to escape being judged. These are all ways in which we stay in our comfort zone. These are actions that are familiar to us and therefore bring us a great deal of comfort and security. As long as we aren't forced to leave our comfort zone, our pulse and blood pressure remain normal; we aren't victims of stress, and happily—life goes on as normal.

The moment we are faced with change in our equilibrium, we begin to panic. Now we must introduce new activities and responsibilities that do not fit into our comfortable lifestyle. The old issues of doubt, fear and procrastination begin to surface. Immediately we fear our ability to succeed, and doubt that we could, even if we tried. So what do we do? We retreat—we simply put things off, and in some instances we do nothing at all.

In order to make ourselves feel better about our behavior, we rely on our excuses. Better yet, we lie to ourselves to give credence to the fact that we are procrastinating. How can we move past this debilitating behavior? It is imperative that we institute change. When implementing change, we must give ourselves a specified amount of time to change, and if we do not make the transformation, then we must examine our circumstances and determine whether or not professional help is needed.

Another method would be to start by analyzing the problem. Set goals for change and take small steps in your goal plan that are attainable. Once you succeed in your initial efforts, give yourself praise and reward. Recall your victories to help you move forward through the list of goals, so that change becomes imminent. This constant reminder of your successes is reinforcement that you can do it; you can set goals and implement a plan of action. Before you know it, your new behavior will take on the attributes that you desire. You will feel secure with new activities and responsibilities. As a result, you become comfortable stretching yourself to new expectations.

Just knowing that you are qualified, capable and able to make great strides is enough to catapult you into new and uncharted territory. You will gain such confidence in your accomplishments, that you will cease to fear change. You will no longer look upon your old comfort zone as status quo. You will begin to welcome change as a new and refreshing frontier, and the best part is you will no longer be held hostage by procrastination.

To further validate what power reflecting on past successes has in helping to move you past procrastination, Dr. Whiting shares his own personal views. "For me it is essential to reflect on past successes if I am doing something and I am struggling with it. For example, I constantly say, 'Come on Cecil, you have done it before—you can do this!' Basically, what I am doing is giving myself some verbal reinforcement. Anything that you tell yourself that is affirming is important, because it keeps you going."

Perfection—Harmful or Helpful?

A controlled study of procrastinators revealed that the majority of those studied were perfectionists. Two-thirds confessed that they were perfectionists; the other one-third didn't realize that their behavior was indicative of being a perfectionist. Perfectionists are those people who strive to do something absolutely flawless at all cost. They often feel they have something to prove.

These individuals often find that they feel overwhelmed regarding the task facing them, primarily because they place themselves in unrealistic situations. They expect far too much of themselves than is actually attainable. When they become aware of their limitations, they become discouraged and withdraw completely. You generally find them waiting for the ideal time to arise so that they can resume the project. In the interim, they utilize all of the necessary excuses afforded them to keep from moving forward and tackling the project.

In the midst of this is denial, self-doubt, fear, and the ultimate outcome—procrastination. Ego definitely gets in the way of rational thinking on the part of a true perfectionist. In trying to understand the thought process of a perfectionist, you can't help but wonder, once perfectionists realize their limitations, why they don't acknowledge the fact that they have limitations, and seek assistance? It's simple—they do not want to be viewed as a failure. The perfectionists' perception of their capabilities is clearly out of proportion!

I think we should strive for perfection, but we should accept a variant. Perfection is programmed distraction, and pre-involvement with perfection is a symptom of perfectionism. This means that you must have everything in order before you can take the next step. Keep in mind that doing a good job should be the emphasis, not perfection. When you go beyond doing the best job that you can, and you try to infuse perfection, at that point you are wallowing in doubt, and doubt will overcome you.

— Dr. Cecil Whiting

No Substitutes Will Do

There is no *middle of the road* business with perfectionists. Conditions must be ideal and the outcome of their efforts must dictate excellence; otherwise, there is no deal. If the situation has any imperfections whatsoever, then perfectionists choose to wait. Remember, these people think they are outstanding at whatever they do, and the seal of approval validating that fact is figuratively stamped across their foreheads.

They want everything in their lives to be ideal. As we all know, life has its twists and turns, and adversity is just a part of the process. Perfectionists don't even begin to know the meaning of the words alternate, substitute, variable, or Plan B. For them their vocabulary consists of: _It's business as usual, everything is status quo, and above all, if I can't get the job done, no one else can!_

One character trait that was expressed by the study group of procrastinators, and I must say their honesty was quite surprising, was that the majority of them enjoyed doing things themselves and being in control. This meant that they didn't have to worry about someone else rocking the boat.

They also admitted that they knew nothing about delegating for success, primarily because they were too afraid that they couldn't count on the other person to bring the spirit of excellence to the project. If it didn't get done by them, it wouldn't be done in the excellent manner to which they had been accustomed, whether real or imagined.

This thinking creates problems for perfectionists. When it is time to seek help, they refuse to do so. That's when the real procrastination starts. You see them start to put things off, and ultimately abandon the project entirely.

Most perfectionists are closet procrastinators. They will take on a project and have you thinking everything is under control, while secretly, they rue the day they ever got involved. The sad commentary is that they won't let you help them with damage control. They are too ashamed to let you know that the project was more than they could handle. Consequently, they carry out this facade of having everyone involved thinking that things are going along as planned. One frustrating thing about dealing with perfectionists is that they see things only one way—theirs. Can you break the habits of a true perfectionist?

Perfectionists must be shown that there is no *absolute* way to do any one thing. To illustrate your point, take a project and identify the end goal; then explain to them what you hope to accomplish after all tasks have been completed. Outline several techniques or methods that can be applied that will yield the desired results. The perfectionists can then see that a plan can have different variables; however the end result remains the same.

Once the point is proven, you can move on and take each plan and dissect it to demonstrate the degree of efficiency within each plan. Ask them to examine the following questions: *Was there more than one way to accomplish the goal? Which plan saved the most time and money? Did the plan suffer as a result of team work?* This exercise will encourage perfectionists to embrace alternative methods, and will get them to accept working with others in problem solving.

In working with perfectionists on a project, be sure to let them know that their contribution to the project was extremely valuable; however, working together, communicating, and being a good team player positively enhanced the outcome of the project.

Elementary as it may seem, this exercise helps the perfectionist to open up to accepting change, asking for help, and understanding the magnitude of a project, and where they fit in with respect to their knowledge and expertise. Ultimately, perfectionists will start to place realistic expectations on themselves. Simply stated—they won't bite off more than they can chew.

5) The Acceptance Principle

We hold the power to control the degree of influence others will have over our decision making. We relinquish control when we place far too much value on their opinion of what we choose to do.

In a recent study, the majority of those who participated acknowledged that a number of their fears stemmed from the fact that they placed far too much value on what others would think of them, and whether they would approve of what they were doing, or even find it acceptable. Their fears caused them to procrastinate and to doubt their ability to make good decisions. As a result, they often found themselves reconsidering their plans, and in some cases abandoning their ideas all together.

Procrastination can rob you of your goals and dreams. To postpone or alter your plans based upon the opinion, approval or acceptance of someone else may cause you to miss out on a rich and rewarding life experience.

The need for advice, approval, acceptance and the opinion of others has been determined to be a major cause of procrastination. One individual in the group confided that the mere thought of what others thought of him nearly scared him to death. When he found himself feeling this way, he refused to act on his plans. He doubted whether there would be a positive outcome. It wasn't until he learned how to control the issues causing doubt, fear and procrastination that he could move forward with confidence.

Some of the stronger personalities in the group had difficulty confessing that this was indeed a concern for them as well. Even in a controlled group where these issues were being explored in a non-threatening environment, some individuals found it extremely embarrassing to admit that they struggled with these issues. After developing a level of comfort within the group, they confessed that part of the problem originated from wanting people to think they had it all together, which, in essence, validated the point that they placed too much value on the opinion of others.

In order to make the study a success, a foundation had to be laid. They admitted that the purpose of the study was to examine procrastination by looking at some of the chief causes. Each member of the group vowed to listen with an open mind and without judgment or prejudice.

An amazing occurrence took place: They began to shed their egos and insecurities. Members of the group began to open up and discuss how they had allowed procrastination to rob them of their joy. As individual members of the group spoke, you could see others nodding their heads in agreement. They were amazed to discover that people from all walks of life shared similar life experiences.

They discovered that issues such as getting advice from others, gaining the acceptance or approval of others, as well as worrying about the opinion of others, were causes of doubt, fear and procrastination.

Advice From Others

A wise man will hear, and will increase learning; and a man of understanding shall attain unto wise counsels: — Proverbs 1:5

There is a point in one's life where the advice from another individual may prove to be quite beneficial. The key is knowing how to decipher when the information or advice is helpful or harmful. Advice should be viewed as a subjective process. Careful examination should be given to a number of issues:

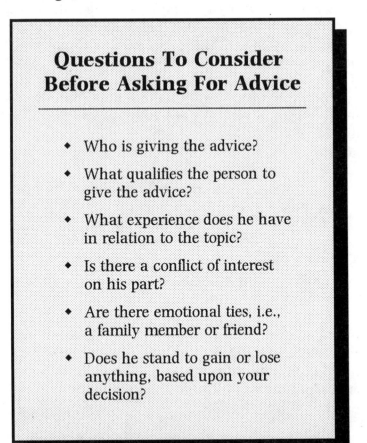

Questions To Consider
Before Asking For Advice

- ◆ Who is giving the advice?

- ◆ What qualifies the person to give the advice?

- ◆ What experience does he have in relation to the topic?

- ◆ Is there a conflict of interest on his part?

- ◆ Are there emotional ties, i.e., a family member or friend?

- ◆ Does he stand to gain or lose anything, based upon your decision?

It is imperative that you make decisions based upon wisdom and knowledge, and not from your emotions. When you select someone as an advisor who is close to you, or who has strong emotional ties, such as a family member or friend, you may accept his or her advice based upon the emotional connection. You may find yourself struggling to rationalize the validity of the advice by going over it in your mind: "Perhaps what my wife said is true; after all, she loves me and wouldn't steer me wrong."

That argument may be true, or at least, true in part. No doubt your wife does love you and has your best interest as heart, however, that may not necessarily qualify her to give you the best advice. Her advice to you may be based upon her emotions.

Let's say for the sake of argument, that you wanted to start a part-time computer business, and base it in your home. You work a full-time job with lots of overtime; your wife has hinted in the past that you spend far too much time working, and less and less time with her and the children. She has no frame of reference with respect to computers or the needs in the market place for your field of specialty.

She views the new addition in your life—the business—as another object vying for your time. Even though you are looking at the opportunity as a plus for the entire family unit, given the additional income, she may view it as a problem. Her advice to you regarding whether or not you should start the business may be based on her emotions.

Prior to seeking others for advice or information, consider the following: Do you have a frame of reference regarding the subject, to be able to compare what the advice giver (the person whom you have designated as the authority) is telling you? How well do *you* know the subject matter? Can you articulate in your own words what your mission is? This will give you a clearer picture of what you hope to gain from the other person's knowledge and expertise. It is important to note that you must conduct some research on your own prior to opening the floor for advice from others.

Make a list of all the questions you wish advice on and give careful consideration to each question. Once the advice has been given, spend some time considering the pros and cons of what has been said. Weigh the issues and decide whether or not you plan to implement the advice into your plans.

At best, there is still some danger in seeking the advice of "experts." We often think that because people have credentials in a given field, they are qualified experts on all phases of the subject. We feel they will absolve our fears because they hold the keys—knowledge and expertise. If your fears are based solely upon lack of knowledge and expertise, then it is time you push ahead full throttle and do your homework. The more knowledge you have, the less you will fear your decisions with respect to that particular subject. Remember, fear is born out of ignorance and lack of knowledge. Knowing that you have acquired sufficient knowledge on the subject should help you relinquish your fears, and above all, give some credence to your ability to make decisions that are good for you.

You must examine your fears, doubts and concerns with regard to what it is you want to do, as opposed to the wishes of others. Ask yourself, why do I need advice from this person? You must decide whether it is truly advice you are seeking rather than approval. There is a difference. How you respond to their input will be based largely on what you are seeking, be it advice or approval.

Getting Approval—Yours, Mine and Ours

Getting approval and getting advice are clearly two separate and distinct issues. When you are in the *approval mode*, you are generally hoping that you'll gain the acceptance or approval of an individual.

When you are in the *advice mode*, your main motivation should be to gain valuable information based upon the individual's knowledge and expertise in a specific field of specialty.

A number of fears are based on the issue of acceptance or approval. As young children we desire to please our parents and loved ones. We are often rewarded for exhibiting acceptable behavior. Our parents show their approval in many different ways. They may reward us with praise or through something more tangible such as a toy or a favorite dessert.

We begin to crave reward and praise—it feels good, and we continue this behavior hoping to gain approval and acceptance throughout our lives. Often we find ourselves transferring this behavior when we interact with our peers and others in social settings. Much to our surprise, as adults we see this behavior finding its way into the work force, as well as into other interpersonal relationships. We simply transfer our desire for approval and acceptance from our parents to other individuals who hold important positions in our lives.

It is easy to see why this type of conditioning is hard to let go. It feels good to receive recognition, reward and praise. We tend to measure what we do by the approval or acceptance of others. When we fear that we will not get it, we are inclined to doubt whether or not we have made good choices. This doubt often leads to procrastination. Before we move forward, we find ourselves vacillating back and forth in hopes that we will get some kind of sign that everything will be all right.

Careful examination needs to be given to the issue of placing such importance on whether people approve of what we do. We must be honest with ourselves when we ponder the question: "Do I hope to gain their approval?" If the answer is yes, then we must examine why we feel it is so important that they approve of what we do. Will their approval enhance or improve the situation? "People who are insecure need the approval of others. I think of _approval_ in much the same way I think of _getting permission_. I only think of permission in relation to working for someone else where permission may be needed to carry out your job," stated clothing entrepreneur Winter Knottingham.

Forms of Approval

Active approval: Active approval occurs when you pose a question and the response is given in a physical or verbal manner. The answer is either yes or no, you don't have to guess about it. For example, a child asks his parent for permission to go swimming, his mother turns and nods her head (physical gesture) as she verbally says yes.

Passive Approval: Passive approval is when you pose a question and the respondent neither agrees nor disagrees and you *assume* that the lack of negative response implies approval. Example: You ask your mother for permission to go to the movies. She is preoccupied with doing something, she turns to you and smiles, never saying yes or no. You may assume from her pleasant disposition that the answer is yes. In fact, she neither verbally approved nor disapproved. Since you wanted approval you chose to acknowledge her smile as a "yes." Passive approval is not expressed or implied approval; it is the personal assumption being derived by the receiving party.

Opinion of Others

There is definitely a difference between advice and opinion. You should not give too much emotional consideration to the opinion of others with respect to what you feel is right for you. Do not spend a great deal of time stressing over what others will think of you. There is a very apropos saying: "What you think of me is none of my business!" Chant the saying to yourself whenever you find yourself struggling with decision making as a result of someone else's opinions of you or what you are doing. Keep in mind that everybody has an opinion, and that your opinion carries as much weight, if not more than others.

Many people want everything to be nice and tidy. They want everyone to like them and approve of everything they do. That kind of thinking isn't practical; this is the real world, and real people do not always agree with each other. What appeals to one may repulse another. Because of these basic differences in likes and dislikes, you can't expect someone else's opinions to always coincide with yours. Coveting the opinions of others causes you to worry. Your worry is fear based and stems from your conditioning and need of approval from others.

A clear identification of your behavioral patterns is needed before you can begin to unravel the nervous anxiety associated with worrying about what others think of you; then you can start making sound decisions for yourself, and move on with your life. How do you get to this point? You must learn how to filter information, and you must learn how to assign value to yourself.

The Filtering Process

As a young child I can recall watching my grandmother sift flour. She was literally separating the unwanted part of the flour from that which was valuable. She only wanted to utilize the pure flour, that which had no lumps or unwanted particles. She used a utensil to help filter out the debris.

We as adults must find a mechanism to filter out the information that is good from that which represents debris. When you listen to people you must do so with what is called a filtering ear. You must take that which is applicable and store it into your mental rolodex and discard the rest. This process becomes especially useful when preventing others from assigning value to you.

Assigning Value

Cassandra Livingston had discovered a need in a specialized market and wanted to write a book to help aspiring hopefuls to become successful. After conducting months of research she completed her book.

While her book was at the printers, she had an opportunity to attend the American Booksellers Convention. This convention is attended by everyone associated with the book trade, from authors, distributors, wholesalers, to buyers of major book chains. There she met an industry leader for whom she had a great deal of respect. She was excited about her new book and began to share her dream of success for her latest work.

Much to her surprise, the gentleman became quite condescending. He said, "While it is admirable that you have written this *little* book, no bookstore will ever carry it. There is just not enough demand for projects like that. You will never get your book into a bookstore!" She was very gracious and thanked him for his opinion.

Because he was an industry leader, she thought about what he had said. Then she stopped abruptly in her tracks and said, "Wait just a minute, that's his opinion of my ability to become successful, not mine. I have done my homework. I have uncovered a need and addressed the issue. I don't need him to validate my work or my ability to become successful!"

Her book came off the press that June. She was invited to appear for book signings by the managers of bookstores in major regional malls across the United States. Some even dedicated the entire window display to her book. She later went on to appear on radio and TV. Her book sold out in November of the same year and went international in the same month. The book sold 30,000 copies immediately and her publisher had to go back to press. *A year later, Cassandra saw that very same industry leader. He knew of her success, and all he could do was smile.*☺

Overcoming Doubt, Fear and Procrastination

What would have happened if she had believed in what he said? She did not need him to define her success or assign value to her—she assigned value to herself. She filtered out all of the debris from the gentleman's advice and relied heavily on her own ability to assign value.

You have the power to circumvent doubt, fear and procrastination brought on by others when you learn how to assign your own value and self-worth. You do not need *anyone* to validate you or your work; simply knowing that you are doing a good job should be validation enough.

You will always rise above the elements when you truly believe in yourself and your ability to become successful. It doesn't matter whether you are writing a book or being the best parent; you must believe that who you are and what you do is valuable. There is a passage that really speaks to this issue:

For it was not an enemy that reproached me; then I could have borne it: neither was it he that hated me that did magnify himself against me; then I would have hid myself from him. But it was a man [my] equal, my guide, and [my] acquaintance.
                                         —Psalms 55:12, 13

6 | *Giving And Taking Control*

Procrastination can be avoided once you understand the process of giving and taking control. Having harmony and balance in your life will be achieved when you can distinguish the difference between delegation and manipulation.

I'm Not Controlled—I'm in Control.

Matthew Wakefield hated it when people would give him instructions. He felt as though they were taking control over his life. Who were they to tell him what to do, was his constant theme. Through therapy he discovered that part of his tendency to procrastinate stemmed from the fact that he was rebelling against authority—people telling him *what to do.*

When he was given orders, or told what to do, Matthew would move at a snail's pace just to usurp authority, and on occasion, he wouldn't respond at all. As a teen, his rebellious behavior caused strained relations with his parents. Instructions would be given to carry out a task, Matthew would acknowledge that he understood and that he would take care of it; instead, he continued to procrastinate.

Reaching the point of being fed up with Matthew's behavior, his parents resorted to reprimanding him, hoping that his guilty conscience would encourage him to complete the task. This method yielded very little success. Matthew would constantly argue with his mother, telling her that guilt trips didn't work on him, and that she and his father could not control his life.

The issue of control plays a major role in the procrastinator's life. Procrastinators who are afraid of losing control, often react by refusing to respond immediately, and by not following through on requests or instructions. To the procrastinators, this behavior demonstrates their ability to take control over a situation. Their tendency to procrastinate does not stem from doubt, it originates out of the fear of losing control. Their theme is, *I'm not controlled—I'm In Control!* They will protect their position at all cost. They take control of a situation and decide when, and if, they will execute a task, ultimately procrastinating just to prove their point.

Giving And Taking Control

With understanding, procrastinators may see that what is taking place in the relationship is a natural progression of day-to-day duties and responsibilities being assigned, rather than someone trying to manipulate and control them.

Taking Control Doesn't Always Mean You're Procrastinating.

There is a clear distinction between people who use procrastination to prove the point that they are in control, and those who refuse to respond to manipulative stimuli. There is truth to the fact that people will try to manipulate and control others through many means; two common themes are guilt and shame. Some parents are notorious for trying to evoke these feelings from their children, often resulting in their unwillingness to let go of the umbilical cord.

Even your friends will try to influence you to come over to their way of thinking through trying to make you feel guilty. Many husbands and wives use this tactic as a form of control. Taking a stand to prevent someone from trying to use shame and guilt to manipulate you, does not mean that you are a procrastinator.

This form of behavior in a relationship demonstrates the desire of one individual to control another. The goal is to keep you *in your place* through utilizing guilt as the motivating factor. Recognize it for what it is worth, and don't be afraid to face it head on. In this instance, it is your responsibility to take control.

In taking control, your job is to gain an understanding of the people you interact with and what is taking place in the relationship. Think of yourself as an author writing a book about guilt, and the experiences you are having. List all of the characters in the plot, and then list their relationship to each other. Outline the main plot and any sub-plots. Identify who has control in each situation and why they have control. Consider what would happen if you relinquished your control of the situation. Who would become the benefactor of that control? Upon closer scrutiny of the situation, ask yourself if you do decide to take back the control, what would be the outcome? What are the pros and cons in regard to your position in the main plot and each sub-plot?

Examining guilt from a non-threatening view makes it easier to get to the bottom of the problem. More often than not, we allow our emotions to cloud the issue. It is easier to put things into perspective when you commit to paper. With the preceding exercise you can see the connection each character has, one to the other, and the degree of their importance. It helps to sort out controlling themes within relationships.

It is important to remember to acknowledge when your behavior is a result of being blatantly manipulated, or when you are using the defense of being controlled to allow you to continue to procrastinate.

Delegate for Success—Giving Control to Others.

Successful people know the art of delegating for success—giving control to others. They clearly understand that they cannot do it all, and are wise to divvy up the workload. This prevents them from feeling overwhelmed, which often leads to procrastination.

When you delegate responsibility to others, you must relinquish a certain degree of control. "This sounds easy in theory," stated Randy Ashcroft, a New York executive. "My problem is that I know if I do the job myself, it is going to get done correctly and on time. When I give control to others, I have a constant worry about whether they are going to do the assignment properly. Over the years, I have learned that I need to carve out a niche of time to give control to others; first to explain the task or job; second, to make sure they understand it; third, to give them time to make their own mistakes; and fourth, to help them correct those mistakes.

Successful Leaders Delegate

After observing their progress, I can gain a level of comfort and confidence to let them go and accomplish the task independently."

Truly successful people seem to have a good understanding of how to delegate, and what to delegate. What is even more impressive is their ability to get qualified personnel to do the job. In a random study of successful individuals, I asked:

What are Your Views on Delegating to Become More Successful?

Jerrold Curry: I would delegate basically everything but the final decision. I think in business the only thing I wouldn't delegate is the ability to sign checks, to cut hours on a time card, and to handle anything that involves money. Delegating frees my time; that's work that I don't necessarily need to do.

Carlease Burke: I'm really creative, and in a perfect world, if I could have everything in my life that wasn't creative taken care of, then that's what I would delegate. I'm talking everything from phone calls to housekeeping. If I could delegate all of that *stuff* and all I had to do was be creative, that would be a perfect world.

Hillary Burton: I would like to delegate the job of a salesperson. I think we need to get someone who is good at selling, because that is neither of our strong points. I think it would increase the business a lot.

Peter Burton: I would like to have it similar to an orchestra and conductor relationship. I would like to get quality instruments going, sit back and conduct.

***Hillary* Burton:** That's what we're striving for; I believe that's the only way you can have a successful business. The players in the business are orchestrated by someone who can see the whole picture.

Gail Taylor Walton: I would delegate more of the planning. That really eats up my time: planning and figuring out methods. It's easy to do something once you've been told exactly how to do it. I need to start leaving some of those details to other people, and have them figure out how to do the job and get back to me. Even if they come back with something I don't exactly want, at least I've given them a chance to express themselves. I can work from their ideas, or I can re-work the plan.

I can remember being left alone in a little room with something and being given extremely skimpy instructions. In fact, the only instructions I was given were along the lines of what the end result was to be. It was up to me to figure out how to get there.

Dr. Cecil Whiting: It is overwhelmingly important to delegate for success. One of the ways to get over the fear of delegating is to give a person an assignment and see how it comes back. If it comes back half-complete, then you've got a problem. If it comes back complete, then you have obtained the results you wanted. If it comes back complete plus, then you have the person you need. You need to hang on to that person at all cost. That's the person who will take your ideas and concepts and bring them to fruition.

John Clemons: The area that I need the most help with is my own busy work. I need an administrative assistant or a secretary, somebody that will think the way I do. For me to be more productive I've got to find the person that can help organize me.

Mary Kay Schreiber: The process wasn't difficult, but getting the right people was. Everybody functions differently. Don't use yourself as a scale, but know that everybody has to be managed differently.

Your role becomes less involved and more of actual management. I segmented everything, and then chose the right person. Part of delegating is being able to distinguish who is right for what job. I think that successful people are able to keep a lot more going at one time than the average person.

In the last two years I finally said, "I am not going to kill myself, I've got to let go. Either I am going to let go, or I am not going to do this anymore, because I am going to explode!"

Leadership

You can avoid procrastination once you understand the process of giving and taking control. You must also learn to become effective when delegating for success and never fear the role of leadership. This applies in both your personal and professional life.

The fear of leadership stems from the need to be accepted and liked by all. It is impossible to win a popularity vote from everyone with whom you interact. Due to varying opinions on how things should be done, you are bound to receive some resistance.

Being an effective leader requires a good balance between giving and taking control. It further requires a good command of communication skills. How effective are you at getting your point across? Do you speak with authority, or when you give specific instructions do you make it sound almost as if you are apologizing? Leadership is an art as well as a skill, make no mistake about it.

People respond to the signals you give, both verbal and physical (your body language). If your demeanor is weak and you come across as being insecure, then you should expect little or no respect from those you are trying to lead. How can they respect and have confidence in you when you have very little confidence in yourself?

People want to know that those in charge have a good command of things and know just where they're going and how to get there. They respect strong, confident leaders and will respond by giving them the respect they deserve.

This does not mean that you have to be a know-it-all, but you are expected to be prepared, and when an issue arises that needs further research, you are expected to know where and how to get the answers. More importantly, you must know how to appease the troops while doing so!

On a personal note: Some heads of households take on more than their fair share of duties for the upkeep and maintenance of the home, rather than risk complaints and confrontations with family members. They clearly suffer from a fear of delegating duties and taking control. They must learn to ignore the moans and groans from family members and stand firm in their ability to delegate duties and responsibilities. They must also assume the position of leadership and set guidelines on how family members are to interact with them. They must stress that there will be consequences to bear, if family members do not accept and carry out their responsibilities.

Good leaders must function in the workplace as well as in their own personal environment. You don't have to act as a dictator at home, but you must get your point across as to what you expect from the family members and what they can expect from you. You want to have harmony in your home and this is one way to achieve it.

How Do You Overcome Your Fear of Leadership?

For the answer to this question, I queried Dr. Cecil Whiting: The process of one feeling comfortable as a leader is the process of *demystification*. Once you can demystify systems and understand that systems tend to work in spite of your lack of understanding of how they work, then you can become part of those systems.

Mentoring is part of the process we go through as leaders. The mentor is the person who has scoped out the organization of any system, who knows the components of that system, and who can share it with someone else. If someone is building a building, the mentor can tell him which contractors come first, what the pitfalls are, and what kind of density the concrete needs. The mentor, in essence, can demystify and dissect the organization that goes into the building process. One of the tools that leads to being less fearful of leadership is *mentoring*.

7) *Are You Afraid Of Success?*

Be not afraid when one is made rich, when the glory of his house is increased.

— Psalms 49:16

Success is chronicled by many things: One's performance and ability to achieve, one's determination, self-confidence, and so on. The real measure of success is subjective; it is what you utilize to measure and place value on yourself, be it real or imagined. People's perception of success greatly impacts their natural ability to succeed.

On your journey to success, one vital element remains paramount among the rest: You do not need the permission of others in order to proceed with your goals.

Permission From Others

Have you ever wondered why you ask other people what they think about something *you* want to do? Do you really need their permission to validate what you want to do? Do you lack the courage or self-confidence in your ability to make good decisions? Some people feel safe sharing decision making with others; waiting for the other person to give them the go-head makes them feel more comfortable. If their plan goes awry, they can always rely on sharing the blame with someone else. This kind of behavior is indicative of someone who is suffering from low self-confidence. Regardless of your reasoning, needing permission from others can cause you to procrastinate. Getting their permission is the same as allowing others to assign value to you and what you wish to do. You must assign value to yourself; you do not need others to assign value to you.

When embarking on a new endeavor, in order to prevent failure, you need to do some research, better known as doing your homework. Part of that process may involve enlisting the knowledge and expertise of those who have experience in that particular field. This does not mean that you need to ask them for permission to proceed with the project. It does mean that you will gather information which will allow you to make intelligent decisions for yourself.

There is definitely a difference between doing your homework to gain information, and asking others if it is okay for *you* to proceed. It must be remembered that in the former example you are investigating to compile information for decision making, not to obtain permission. Be honest with yourself, and make sure it is the information you seek, rather than permission.

When you seek out specific individuals for their knowledge and expertise, some feel inclined to offer their opinion about your ability to become successful. Take it with a grain of salt. Realize that they do not know your full potential, and therefore may make value judgments based on superficial observations of what they perceive to be your capabilities.

When you are researching a new venture, there are many variables of which you may be unsure. This uncertainty may appear to the other person as inadequacy, or lack of the ability to function in that capacity. It is amazing how those who have *arrived* find it so easy to forget how they got there! They, too, started from a point where they needed to inquire about the "ins and outs" of a new venture.

Giving others the power to give you permission to go forward is dangerous. Do not jeopardize your success by becoming *permission dependent*. You do not need their permission as you take the helm on your journey to success. While it may feel good to your ego to have it, remember, you don't need it to go forward.

This may sound somewhat conceited, nevertheless, it is imperative that you maintain a level of confidence for your own well-being. You must have that winner's attitude, and that *I can do it* spirit. Some people look at positive-thinking individuals and say, "Boy, they think they're hot stuff." Well, they had better, if they want to get anywhere in life. Do not allow your confidence to be shaken by someone criticizing your spirit of self-confidence. If left unguarded, people will tear it down in less than a fraction of the time it took to build.

Giving Yourself Permission

The argument for giving yourself permission is equally as strong as it is for not getting permission from others. The road to success is traveled by those who realize the benefit in giving themselves permission to pursue their dreams. Far too often people depend upon the thoughts and well-wishes of others. It's hard to fully convey your passions to someone who has no frame of reference. The harder you try, the more you buy into believing that their approval is paramount.

If you are looking for that *seal of approval* to come from someone other than yourself, you will be greatly disappointed. Why give that kind of power to another individual?

You must embrace the belief that your decisions carry a great deal of merit. Your belief in yourself and your capabilities has to be strong enough to survive the input of individuals who simply can't appreciate your goals.

Getting permission can be a "feel good" experience; however, giving yourself permission feels better. You cannot be held hostage to the desires of others. You must rely on your own ability to penetrate the rudimentary emotions that make you feel good. Once tapped, you can visit as often as you like.

Standing on your own two feet, taking full responsibility for your success means a complete overhaul of your thought process. Learning to give yourself permission may be a foreign concept at first. Chant the following to yourself as permission reinforcement: *I do not need to get approval, advice or consent from anyone other than myself!* Attitude reconditioning is the first step in getting to the point where permission becomes singular rather than plural.

What Character Traits Do Successful People Have?

The following successful individuals share their thoughts on the character traits successful people should possess. To learn more about these dynamic individuals turn to chapters eight and nine.

Pat Tobin: Certainly, a good attitude helps, because people want to do business with people they like. If you turn people off, you're not going to be very successful. You need to have a good attitude, care about others, and be unselfish. You have to be willing to give to get something back—give of yourself, your time, and your resources; those are the kind of things that I think are important.

Mary Kay Schreiber: They must have passion. I see that in most people who are successful—somehow passion runs ribbons through their success. They are multi-talented and multi-faceted. You can't only be good in one area to be successful. You have to be able to deal with a lot of different areas to keep it up and running. You also need to have a stick-to-it attitude, be very centered, and constantly search for excellence within yourself.

Pastor Dave Stoecklein: They know how to set goals and seek out steps to get there; they set priorities and keep them. They get the most out of the time, money, or possessions that they have.

Carlease Burke: The qualities of most successful people include tenacity, persistence, having a positive outlook on life as well as having a positive self-image, being a self-starter, being able to take charge and do things, and being able to own their own power and not worry about what other people say. They must be good at delegating, communicating and networking. They don't allow people to talk them out of what's in their heart. I don't think successful people are ever finished.

Jerrold Curry: I believe success requires having a hard drive and a willingness to succeed. You acquire that by just wanting something out of life. Not everybody wants something. Some people are content with being nothing or just making it day-to-day.

Don Price: After taking a look at what makes people successful, I discovered that there are about five principles. _Who you know and who knows you_, that's the first principle. The second principle is that _your success comes from mobilizing the power of others around you._ The third principle is _luck and opportunity._ Number four is to _become a power networker._ It is not a matter of going out and seeing how many business cards you can distribute everyday, but how many relationships you can build and have those relationships work in your favor. The fifth principle is that you have to be creative and innovative in anything you do today in order to climb the corporate success ladder, build a business, or sell yourself.

Dr. Jane Myers Drew: They know themselves; they accept themselves. They listen to their inner guidance so they know the right direction for them to go. Success is defined by the person.

Gail Blake-Smith: Successful people have very good self-esteem and an excellent faith-value system, knowing that failure isn't the end of everything; it is just a test or a tool to help us grow. It may be a detour in finding other avenues in how to get somewhere. Success is looking for the best in people, trying to be understanding, as opposed to always being understood, and being persistent.

S. Barry Hamdani: Successful people have very similar character traits. We value our time and that of others. We listen closely to people we respect. We offer something to others before we request something. We are not afraid to ask for directions or suggestions. We are very sensitive to success and failure because we put our hearts into our work. We maintain relationships with other successful people over distance and time because we feed off the same bread of thought and ideas.

Roberta Pierce: I think people tend to measure success by money—I don't. To me success is operating with ethics. It's being 110 percent committed to your objective. It's never stepping on someone else to get where you want to be. It's believing in yourself with all your heart.

Hillary Burton: One of the qualities that a successful person has is the ability to prioritize, knowing

99

what's important, what has to get done, in both areas of life, personal and professional and keeping them in sight. Success is keeping your priorities ahead of you and starting the day with a prayer.

Lisa Valore: A successful person has the appearance of confidence, a professional demeanor, the ability to listen and respond, and is organized. Organization and good communication skills are important keys to success.

John Clemons: Initiative is the main ingredient needed to reach success. Don't wait for someone else to show you or to do it for you. You must figure out how to do it. I personally think a little luck helps.

Derek Scott: Success includes having sound values and goals, being people oriented, honest, trustworthy and fair. You must be able to communicate, delegate and lead well. A good sense of humor, a can-do attitude and determination are important ingredients that go into the recipe that turns out a successful and happy person.

Trapped By the Fear of Failure

I look around at my neighbor; she seems to be fortunate at everything she does. It's easy for her, she is married and doesn't have to depend on herself for food, shelter and clothing. I, on the other hand, am single with two kids in college, working for the county and am up to my ears in stress and pressure.

I've contemplated taking my retirement and investing into my dream—owning my own business. With the economy the way it is, I know that isn't practical, especially with several years left before my youngest finishes college. What if I should fail—then what? I need a guarantee that I won't lose the shirt off my back.

I know that I am good at what I do. It's just too hard to start a new business at my age.

This sounds like the spiel many people chant to themselves. These are people who are trapped by the fear of failure. They have a thousand-and-one excuses why they will fail. You never hear anything in their dialogue that remotely sounds positive. Who wouldn't fail with an attitude like that? You can't get the horses out of the barn if you don't open the door!

If you feel that you have talent and are truly good at what you do, it's quite possible that if you are willing to leave your comfort zone, and push the envelope, you just might succeed. For those of you who are die-hard procrastinators stuck in that preconceived notion of failure, we won't bother to use any old-fashioned clichés such as, _Nothing ventured, nothing gained,_ or, _Nothing beats a failure but a try._

Truly successful individuals are not afraid of failure. They realize the potential exists, however they do not make it an issue. Warren George, an extremely ambitious young man, decided to take on a new career, maintain his current career and embrace yet another, all at the same time. Warren is a consummate fashion designer, one of the most sought after hair artists in the industry, and soon to be owner of a health food restaurant. Talk about someone who is immune to failure, he literally confronts it head-on. That's why he is enormously successful. In an interview, Warren speaks candidly about his success.

Warren, how do you prioritize your life to get things done?

I take it, as they say, step-by-step. I do a lot of writing everyday. I write in my journal everyday. I go through a legal pad like a maniac. Not that I get joy out of it. I can't get through life without it.

What is your opinion about putting things off?
It could be very dangerous to continue to procrastinate, because you will fall further and further behind. You are wasting time and could miss your chance to succeed. If you don't take that chance, someone else will. At this time in my life, if I put something off it's usually because I'm too busy to get to it. It's not that I'm sitting around procrastinating and not doing it. It's because I am busy doing other things. There is a huge difference.

As a fashion designer, did you ever worry about your audience accepting you?
I've never had a problem with that. It was just me dealing with me. I was very shy when I was young. I didn't do a lot of things because of shyness. I didn't like attention drawn to me.

How did you overcome your shyness?
I forced myself. I started when I was younger. Instead of going to an analyst, I did it the cheap way—I just went out there. Modeling helped a lot.

You seem very confident in yourself. Are there times when people intimidate you?
The older I get, the less people intimidate me. My confidence is up. It plays a major role. I'm planning to buy a restaurant. It's a health food restaurant where I used to work in 1978. It has just been thrown my way. I went to a conference with some investors. Everyone was looking at me and listening to my ideas. I enjoyed it. I knew exactly what I wanted because I did my homework. I was prepared. It was really interesting.

You weren't nervous?

I had no problem, I enjoyed it. I think it really counts when you know what you are talking about. That helps you overcome challenges. Plus, I look at people as just being people. Everyone is playing a role. The marketing person is playing a role, so that is the way I look at it. Being prepared, recognizing who your audience is, and not allowing them to intimidate you will be to your advantage. The preparation especially helps me not to feel intimidated.

Do you know the restaurant business?

Actually, I do. When I was twenty I managed a health food restaurant. From 1978 to 1982, I worked with my sister at the restaurant that has been offered to me; she was the manager. The owners we worked for left, and the present owner is not able to run it. I have a history with that place. That's why I'm negotiating with the investors.

My sister and I are planning to operate the restaurant together. I'm giving her a percentage of the profits. If I do hair three days a week, that income will support me, and we can build the restaurant. My sister has six years' experience in the restaurant business. Her name is Christine, so we're going to call the restaurant *Christine.*

Would you say you have been successful?

I have been successful at going after what I set out to do. When I get old I can say that I did that, not that I made money, but I did it. That's important to me.

When did you realize you have talent as a designer and as a hair artist?

I have always had an interest in hair. At fashion shows I would sit backstage watching the hair artists style the models' hair. I was amazed by it. As a fashion designer, cutting fabric has allowed me to work with my hands. After cutting fabric for so many years, I wasn't afraid to cut hair. If you have been cutting silk as long as I have, you can cut hair. You are able to look at lines; I think that your eyes become trained.

You are saying it is easy to transfer skills from one discipline to another?

Yes. It is the experience that you carry with you. When I was in hair apprenticeship I was able to draw from my experience in fashion design. It's a road that I've already traveled; I just moved from fabric to hair.

You had no trepidation whatsoever?

Not at all. Not even when I went to my first hair salon, a very popular salon in Los Angeles on Melrose Boulevard. I had just obtained my cosmetology license. The other stylists had five, ten, and even twenty years' experience styling the hair of celebrities. I learned a lot from them.

I went to another salon and worked for minimum wage as an assistant to learn the art of cutting. I returned to Melrose after a year-and-a half of sweeping floors, working as an assistant and earning minimum wage. From this experience I learned that the only person you should compete with is yourself. You cannot worry about what someone else is thinking or saying about you. If you have to work backwards making less, do it. Nothing lasts forever. It is temporary, and it's worth it if you're learning and improving. I learned confidence by hanging in there and not giving up.

What character traits do successful people have?

The successful people I have seen are serious about their work. They seem to almost be workaholics.

When they go for it, they go for it all the way. They are passionate about what they do. I believe they love the drive and the endurance.

Are you as equally successful in your personal life?

At this point, success in my personal life comes from the success in my professional life. So everything is universal.

You challenge so many things, would you say you are a risk taker?

Yes; and I am not afraid to lose. If I lose, I'll just start from the bottom again and go back to the top. I am sure it won't take that long, because I am much more experienced in getting back to the top. I take all of the negatives and turn them into positives.

Do you accept advice from other people?

I always listen to advice. I take it and then analyze it. Sometimes I act on the advice just to see if it's applicable to me.

What advice do you have for overcoming doubt, fear and procrastination?

Evaluate yourself to see what is good and what is bad; then work on what is bad. Just go for it—do it. I think that is the best advice: Just do it!

Confidence Course

During the mid-eighties, I taught two challenging courses, *Human Dynamics* to my eager new freshmen, and *Professional Development* to my departing college seniors. I use the term challenging, because my job was to prepare one group—college seniors—to enter the work force, and to help another—college freshmen—discover their real potential.

Both classes required the students to establish a level of comfort with respect to their abilities. To achieve the goal of elevating their confidence and self-esteem, I would have them work through an intensive exercise called the "No Principle." The basis of the exercise is to strengthen one's ability to give themselves permission to go forward and become successful. This process is accomplished by eliminating negative emotional stimuli and reinforcing positive thinking. A very significant element of the exercise is to teach how to de-junk the subconscious mind.

Until you are comfortable giving yourself permission, you may require a great deal of deprogramming. To reach a point where you feel secure with your position as the permission giver, the following exercise can help. The exercise is designed to take you from permission dependency to permission superiority. It takes you from a plural state of mind to a singular form of being—an interdependency on oneself.

Elevating Your

Self-Confidence

and

Self-Esteem

It is interesting to note that both groups of students had much of the same concerns in common. They both needed to give themselves permission to become successful. The college freshmen needed to give themselves permission to get to the position of the college seniors; and the college seniors needed to give themselves permission to take their hard-earned knowledge into the career marketplace. Both groups had the tendency to look beyond themselves for permission, when in fact, the irony of the story is that they both held the key to success within themselves.

The "No Principle" Exercise

To participate in this exercise you will need paper and pen, a quiet location and the willingness to follow through. Start by getting totally relaxed. Take your shoes off and loosen any restricting clothing. Before being seated, stretch your body, then rotate your neck to relieve any tension of the day. Make sure the lighting is conducive for relaxation. Make a list from the following example.

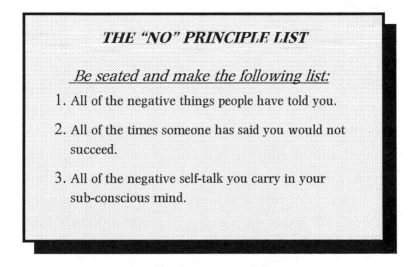

THE "NO" PRINCIPLE LIST

Be seated and make the following list:

1. All of the negative things people have told you.

2. All of the times someone has said you would not succeed.

3. All of the negative self-talk you carry in your sub-conscious mind.

Once you have completed your list, it's time to stop that old negative tape and replace it with one that reflects positive thinking. You must say to yourself that you are qualified, and you will become successful, and that yours is the only permission needed to move forward.

In a standing position with your eyes closed, stretch your body once again. Take a deep breath and hold it as you count to five, then exhale. Take another deep breath and hold it to count, then exhale. With your eyes continued to be closed, focus on the issues on your list, plant them firmly in your mind. You are centered, you are relaxed, and now you will let go of all the controlling themes represented on your list. Take another deep, cleansing breath, and let go as you count to five. At the count of five you will scream in your loudest voice *NO!*

You are saying *no* to all of the negative things people have told you, to all of the times they have said you would not succeed, and *no* to all of the negative self-talk you have entertained. Once you have released these issues, you will find that the need to be permission dependent will no longer be a problem. Now it is time to put the final closure on the *No Principle;* take your list and crumble it as small as you can and put it where it belongs—in the trash!

You feel exhilarated, because you have crossed over the threshold to permission superiority. You have a new tape in your mental rolodex that says: "I am qualified and able. I will be successful. I am no longer held hostage by needing the permission of others." This exercise builds self-confidence and self-esteem; it gives you the confidence to go forward with a significant degree of belief in your ability to become successful. When my students performed the exercise in a group setting, electricity permeated the atmosphere. Self-confidence and self-esteem is contagious.

Determination Equals Success!

It is a hearty challenge to overcome lifelong issues such as doubt, fear and procrastination. It requires a deep understanding of how these problems affect you, personally. An understanding of the symptoms helps to overcome the obstacles. However, more importantly, a willingness to change must be in place. Old habits are hard to get past. Years of conditioning and programming have to be peeled away, layer-by-layer until you can find the *new you*. Once you have tapped into that total being, there is no turning back. You must reward that deserving human being by being good and kind to yourself. Remember the real joys of life.

The New You

*I am one who lives life to the fullest,
enjoys quiet walks in the park,
gets rejuvenated from
the smell of garden flowers,
and delights in the music
the birds sing.*

*I am one who can wake up to
a morning rain and triumph in
the sounds of soft wind
against the window pane.*

*I am one who can sit by the fire
curled up with a good book
as the cadence of the rain reminds
me how good it is to be alive.
I am one who knows how to meditate
as I gently quiet my soul.*

—Barbara Wright Sykes

8) *Against All Odds—Achieving Success*

From the kitchen to the closet two highly successful people have broken through the barriers of traditional beginnings and have achieved success with nothing but their beliefs and determination.

Pat Tobin

Tobin & Associates, a highly successful PR firm in Hollywood was founded by an undaunted and brave spirit—Pat Tobin. She left a secure job at CBS when her daughter was a teenager to launch her business full-time. *She started out with her typewriter on the kitchen table and her file cabinet right beside it.*

John Clemons

Millions of Americans have learned how to operate their computer software as a result of an ingenious video pioneer—John Clemons. *He started his business out of the closet.* When John started selling his videos, he would go to the post office everyday for three weeks and there would be nothing there; one day he was pleasantly surprised when he opened the post office box, and there was an order.

Pat Tobin

Pat Tobin's story is an inspiring one. She overcame odds many of us have never had to face. Her mother died when she was on the brink of becoming a teenager. She lived with relatives in Philadelphia until she married at the young age of 18. She was a mother at 22 and divorced at 28. Pat studied at Temple University in Philadelphia and the Charles Morris Price School of Advertising and Journalism, where she graduated with honors. Before striking out on her own, Pat served as a marketing representative for Sunoco and worked for Mobil Oil. Upon moving to Los Angeles, she worked as a media coordinator in the entertainment division of CBS Television.

In the early 1970s Pat Tobin became the founder and president of Tobin & Associates, one of the nation's leading African-American owned public relations firms. She left a secure job at CBS when her daughter was a teenager, so she could dedicate full time to her business. *She started out with her typewriter on the kitchen table and her file cabinet right beside it.* Tobin & Associates has developed publicity campaigns for a variety of corporate, civic and community clients. Additionally, they serve as a liaison to politicians, religious leaders, business and professional organizations and the entertainment and sports industries. Tobin & Associates' past and current clients include Toyota Motor Sales, USA., Inc.; Reebok International, Ltd.; Walt Disney Feature Animation; AT&T; and Eastman Kodak Company, to name just a few.

As busy as Pat is, she finds time to spend with her daughter and grandson. She loves to bowl and watch movies. She likes traveling with a group of friends, and enjoys going to Hawaii.

What are the pros and cons of your business?

Let's start with the pros, such as having your own business, and not being fired or being laid off. I don't have to worry about getting a decrease in my pay, because as long as I'm working hard for myself, I can give myself a raise any time, and I do. It is rewarding to know that you can do your own thing; to follow your dream. When you see it become a reality, that is the most rewarding experience there is. During all those years of working for major companies and even CBS Television, I wanted to be in public relations. I spent five years working for CBS Television. I took a leave of absence from CBS in 1983. My daughter was out of high school and I said, "We're on our own now, you've got to get a job, go to college, or do something. The ball is in your court now. There's only the two of us, so we've got to help each other. You've got to help me, and I'm going to help you. I'm going to start my business."

My daughter used to complain about the typewriter on the kitchen table and the file cabinet in the kitchen; but now she says, "Mom, I'm proud of you." She's a publicist for ABC Television Network. She graduated from USC with a degree in communications. She's done well. I'm proud of her.

I don't want to address the cons, but I'll just say this: There are times when you wonder, am I going to have enough to pay this month's overhead, but I've been in business twelve years, and have been in this same building since 1983. I stepped out on faith. It hasn't been easy, anything that is too easy, look out; you don't want it. This has been a long, hard struggle. I thank God I can see clearer everyday that He allows me to continue to grow and succeed.

How did you choose this profession?

I was always putting events together—I was promoting. Actually, I didn't know it was public relations at the time. I married early and divorced early; being a single parent raising a daughter, I couldn't go to a four-year college. Education was always important to me, so going to school at night was what I had to do. I attended The Charles Morris Price School of Advertising and Journalism. I took classes to learn more about advertising and journalism; that's when I realized I was really doing public relations. And now, thank God, today I'm considered a PR practitioner, and I have a full staff.

It is a rewarding feeling knowing that you can set a goal and achieve it. It has not been easy, but nothing worth having is easy. My mother died when I was 12; that's when we came to live in Philadelphia. I was married at 18, a mother at 22, and divorced by the time I was 28.

I got my start in Philadelphia working in the community, in terms of getting into publicity and promotions. I got my start through Reverend Jesse Jackson's PUSH—People Uniting to Save Humanity. Growing up in Philly I was very involved in that organization. They needed a PR person, a communications person.

Have you helped many people break into this business?

I love helping people. I am always glad to encourage and inspire people who want to get into public relations. I'm in the position now where I can do something—reach back and give back, and pull somebody up. I am currently acting as a mentor to Lisa Gordon, whom you met.

Some of those bigger agencies out there are not always so fair and kind; even if they give you an opportunity to get in, some of them will just put you in the mail room and have you sit all day stuffing envelopes. At Tobin & Associates you get an opportunity to interface with clients and actually work at an event. You really have hands-on opportunities.

Those big companies that have hundreds of people still don't give an African-American that same kind of opportunity. It makes me sad, and that is one of the reasons Helen Goss and I started the Black Public Relations Society here in Los Angeles, because there was a need. We are the co-founders. It is a national organization, and I am the national acting-president. It really got started in Chicago in 1983. The Black Public Relations Society was founded by a lady named Sharon Morgan in Chicago. We found out about it, and Helen Goss and I launched the Los Angeles Chapter. Now there are chapters in six cities.

A lot of people who didn't know that there are black PR people can call us. We have a directory of PR professionals. We can always refer somebody, because we are a resource directory. We know where the black professionals are in PR.

A good example: the Mingle Group is a large advertising agency out of New York. The Mingle Group was referred to us a year or so ago. They put on a wonderful event every year in six cities across the country, and Felicia Rashad is the spokesperson—it is perspectives of African-American art. They usually have it at the African-American Museum.

They called us in Los Angeles, and they needed somebody in Detroit. I referred them to a lady in Detroit, and she has had the contract for two years. We have had it for two years here in LA it's just like the *good old boy network* that's been working for so long for other people. Now we have the *good old girl network.*

What are some of your hobbies?

I love to bowl. I was in a bowling league; however, due to the demands on my schedule, I had to give up my bowling, but I'm going to get back into it. Bowling is one of my favorite things.

Movies—I consider going to the movies a hobby. I don't just wait for a special movie to come out, I'll go to see anything. I love going to the movies just to critique and see what's out there—to see how many African-Americans are getting an opportunity to tell their story and do their thing, such as *Waiting To Exhale,* from a black author to a black director, to black actors.

I enjoy comedy. My real fantasy is to be a comedian, not just a stand-up comedian. I like table conversation comedy, where we are just sitting around talking and everybody's laughing—that's my hidden fantasy.

Are successful people exempt from doubt, fear, and procrastination?

Anybody who has lived on this earth has experienced those. Procrastination—I'm guilty of that one. That's why I can't wait to read your book. I don't procrastinate when it comes to my business. But certain things that I don't want to do... every year at tax time; I have the best tax man around, and he has to practically chase me down. I just don't like all the details. Honey, I will be there on April 15th at midnight, the last person trying to mail my taxes.

As you grow, you learn there are certain things you can't change. There's a saying or prayer I like: "God grant me the courage to change the things I can change, the courage to accept the things I cannot change, and the wisdom to know the difference."

I don't think I would be here in business today if I had a lot of fears. There was a little doubt in striking out on my own at first, because I was giving up a secure job with a paycheck, dental plan, eye care, etc. The only way I could be successful and make sure I didn't fail was to try. I keep telling my little three-year-old grandson to keep on trying. He tells me, "Grandma, I can't." I tell him, "Don't use the word, *can't. Can't* is not in your vocabulary."

I paid my dues. I worked for the Olympics in 1984 from 11 pm at night until 7 am in the morning. Then I would leave and come here to run my office. I didn't care if I didn't sleep. So when I tell people success takes a lot of hard work, I've been there.

When you say success, it doesn't always mean money and material things. If you feel good inside about what you are doing and where you are in life, you are successful. I feel good about where I am. I worked long hard hours, and I didn't complain. It was a challenge I had to overcome. It's like a runner—like Wilma Rudolph or Florence Griffith Joyner. If you are going to run that race, you've got to get ready; you've got to practice, and you've got to do whatever it takes. I wanted to own a successful, thriving, growing PR firm. I couldn't sit back and say, *I can't do this.* Hard work is good for you. I had a goal to achieve.

I used to promote the Speakeasy Nightclub on Santa Monica Boulevard. I wasn't a drinker and I didn't run around with men, but this was a way to supplement my income. It was a little promotional thing I did on the side. My daughter, who was a teenager then, would come up there with me some nights; she would wait for me and do her homework. I did that for almost ten years. There were a lot of things I just had to do, and whatever it took to get it done, I did it. I always say now to my associates, "I don't like excuses. I don't care what it takes to get something done, just do it."

Who makes you feel like a success?

I look at my daughter. Everyday I thank God for her and for what she has done. People always say, "That's little Pat Tobin." It makes me feel good; she's done well. She's working for ABC Television. She's a single mother with a three-year old son. I admire what she goes through every day—taking her son to school, picking him up from school, taking him to the doctor, maintaining her job at ABC Television, being on a shoot, being on location, and being at the tapings of the various shows. She works on *Family Matters, Hanging with Mr. Cooper,* starring Mark Curry, and *Champs;* I can't even name all of the shows—she has four or five shows that she does.

Most of the people I come in contact with make me feel like a success; I guess it's the lives that I've been fortunate to touch. There are a couple of people who have worked for Tobin & Associates whom I have watched their growth, and that makes me feel wonderful. I'm very proud of them.

Gretchen Cook interned with Tobin & Associates a few years ago. She is now a professor at Howard University teaching Japanese. When I met her she was just a recent graduate from Spellman College in Atlanta. Then she went on to get her master's degree at John's Hopkins in DC. Torrie O'Neal—Torrie is now the Fund Development Director for Planned Parenthood. She was a college student at Cal State Long Beach, and she worked here at Tobin & Associates for a few years.

I have a thousand dollar scholarship in my name that I give every year. It started two or three years ago. Every year, through the Black Public Relations Society, we have an annual scholarship luncheon, and students who are pursuing a career in PR fill out the application and are considered for the scholarship. I make sure I give back.

Have you ever felt like a failure?

Sometimes things are beyond your control, and things happen for a reason. Getting married at 18 was a big mistake. It's not that I was a failure, I wasn't ready. I have never remarried. Some people tried to discourage me from getting married then, but I wouldn't listen. Time heals all wounds.

What are the major causes of failure?

When it comes to business you may fail if you don't have a good team—good financial and legal guidance, and good associates—you need a good team. Failure can come from not planning properly or having the kind of expertise you need in those different fields, for example, financial and legal needs. The woman who

119

handles my finances is very good at managing money and running a business. She will not let me spend a dime, unless it is accounted for. Sometimes I get a little careless and say, "Give me some money, I need to go do this, that or the other," and she looks at me and says, "I don't think so."

Are you good at giving control to others?

That's hard! I started as a one-woman operation in my kitchen—it's like having a baby. You have people giving you advice, but you have to have your own ideas. When you have people who have different areas of expertise, such as your attorney or accountant, you have to let them take over and handle certain things; but never give too much control. You'll be out of control if you let people take over control of your life.

We've grown tremendously; we have a lot of accounts and I just can't do it all. Teamwork is so important. I'm learning to discriminate and to delegate. I'm getting better.

In some cases people have political relationships that have to be savored because someone else might not understand the protocol.

That's a real good point. I can think of some people like that.

Do you allow others to assign value or self-worth to you?

If someone wanted to buy my business, how can a value be assigned to it, when it took me twenty-five years to build? It is a product of my blood, sweat and tears; I've built it from the ground up.

There was someone who said, "You're going to have a hard time getting corporate accounts." Toyota Motor Sales has been a client since 1987 or 1988.

Toyota pays us good money; they know we work hard. We do what we're supposed to do. We give them good service. We travel around the country with them. I've been to Japan. If they need something by a certain date, it's there. They are one of our anchor clients.

What makes you accept advice from people?

I consider the source. You can't tell me how to do something if you haven't done it yourself or don't know how to do it, or if it's not your area of expertise. I want to do what you're doing one day. I want to write a book. I would never argue with you about writing a book, because I've never written a book. So if Barbara Wright Sykes would say to me, "I need you to understand, Pat, this is how it works; this is how you do your outline, and this is how you do your letter of release," I would say, "Yes, Miss Barbara," because you know.

Does the opinion of others weigh heavily on your mind?

Oh, no. I'm not concerned about what other people think. As long as I'm doing what I think is right, and I'm not doing anything bad, I don't care what they think. If they think, "Pat Tobin works too many hours in that office," and if I need to be in this office to achieve something, then I'm going to be here. I'm very firm about that. I don't care what they think, as long as I'm not hurting anybody else.

Let's recap: You're a single mother, you leave a good paying stable job at CBS to start your own business, (not on a whim). Did anyone ask you if you were crazy?

Oh, yes, some people did say, "Girl, you must be out of your mind." But on the other hand, there were those people who said, "You can do it. I know you'll make it. You're good at it." Ann Kalman, one of the managers at CBS, was very encouraging. When I wanted to take a leave of absence, Mary Kellogg, now the vice-president of Disney, was encouraging. I'll never forget one of the people I admired a great deal, Barbara Harris, now bishop of the Episcopal Church. She said to me, "You want to be the hottest thing in PR by Saturday night." She's helped to steer me to the Charles Mars Price School of Advertising and Journalism. There were people along the way who encouraged me, who guided me, and who gave me good advice. To some I listened; to others I didn't. If anyone was negative or told me I couldn't do it or don't do it, I didn't listen.

I remember a picture of a little red wagon. Under the wagon it said, "Push, pull, or get out of the way." I like to think of myself, not only as a little red wagon, but as a train that will steamroll over you if you don't get out of the way while I'm trying to accomplish something.

Do you feel that if you can't do something perfectly, you won't challenge it at all?

I don't know anyone who is perfect. I've always tried to do my best. If I know someone who can do something better, then I don't mind delegating that project or task. I'm not the best writer in the world, so I will hire personal writers or journalists to assist me in that area of expertise.

I am not an expert at everything. I don't have a problem asking for help. I keep thinking about the associates we have here: Richard Pinnel, who is one of our senior account execs; Lori Reed, who graduated from Clark University in Atlanta; Posh MacIntosh, Kim Jones—I ask for their input and their opinion. I don't think I can do it all, or know it all. I know my limitations. It reminds me of the song that Kenny Rogers sings: "You've got to know when to hold them and know when to fold them."

When do you feel good about yourself?

I'm feeling good about myself all of the time. I'm glad to be alive! Thank God, I have my legs, my arms, and my limbs. Joan Crowner is one of my dearest friends; we've been friends for 27 years. Her mother is ill with cancer, and she is at the point where she has to go to the hospital everyday. Someone has to be with her around the clock. I was talking with Joan the other day, and I started my conversation with: "Girl, I don't feel good. This asthma, this allergy...you know what? Wait. Let me stop. I feel okay. I have felt better, but how is your mother?" Then she started telling me about her mom.

Whatever was bothering me is inconsequential. I'm like the woman who complained about no shoes until she saw someone with no feet. I'm also thinking that I'm like the woman in *Footprints In The Sand*, who asked God, "Where were you when I needed you the most?" And He said, "I carried you when there was only one set of footprints in the sand." I feel good about myself everyday, because He has given me the strength and the courage to do what I need to do.

Things don't always go right. There are going to be days—character-building days—as Les Brown, the motivational speaker, says. I used to say, "I'm having a bad day." I try not to say that anymore; I'm having a character-building day. I thank God for each day—each day is a new day. If you wake up, you are a step ahead.

You have had a number of large corporate accounts. In reading your client list Film Director Spike Lee was also one of your clients. Can you tell me about that relationship?

Spike Lee has certainly been a big inspiration in my life. Spike was another driving force that helped, because I went to work for him on *Do the Right Thing*. Spike said, "We're going to have African-Americans involved in the marketing and promotion of our film."

He made sure we got paid fairly. We didn't just get crumbs off the table. If they were paying a mainstream firm $50,000 to $60,000 a year, his black firm would be paid the same amount.

How did you meet Spike Lee?

That's another story—it's a good story, too. I was at the National Association for Black Journalist Convention. They always show films at the Black Journalists Convention—new films that are coming out. They showed a film called, *She's Got to Have It*. Victoria Horsford was working on *She's Got to Have It* in New York. She is the sister of Anna Marie Horsford (the actress who played the daughter of Sherman Hemsley on the sitcom *Amen)*.

I saw the film, and I came out of the theater talking about the film, so Victoria said, "Pat, they don't have anyone on the West Coast handling PR. Why don't you call Island Pictures and tell them what you can do for them on the West Coast." She was standing there, working with the company, promoting the film, and telling me what to do in order to get involved on the West Coast.

I called Island Pictures. I think Victoria gave me the name of someone named Schwartz. Honey, I got on that phone and I said, "My name is Pat Tobin. I just saw

She's Got to Have It. I know what I can do for you. I know the black press and I know the black community; I know how to get the word out." He said, "Okay, come on in and we'll talk." I sold myself over the phone. I could have said, "Okay, Victoria, I'll call," and never called. So when people say you can't do something, as James Brown says, "I don't want you to give me anything, just open the door. I will get it myself."

I need to have a reunion of all the Tobin & Associates. Kimberly Bailey, a young lady in Las Vegas, went to Spellman. She knew Spike from Spellman-Moorehouse days. We all collaborated, put our little heads together, and got the account.

What advice do you have for overcoming doubt, fear and procrastination?

You can go around them, you can go under them, you can go over them, and you can overcome them! There's no reason not to succeed—you can do it! Just listen to that inner voice, wherever it's coming from. If you're afraid, talk to somebody who's done it.

John Clemons

John Clemons is the founder and president of LearnKey, Inc., publisher of CD-ROM multi-media titles and instructional videos that teach people how to use their computers. LearnKey was born in 1987 when Clemons created an instructional video on how to use WordPerfect. With little research and zero experience in how to market a product of this nature (and keeping his *real* job as a video producer at Brigham Young University), he took out a personal loan to design and print a direct marketing brochure that would be included with WordPerfect software. After three months of waiting and checking the post office box everyday, someone actually ordered and paid for the video. Since that day, LearnKey has steadily increased the number of video titles offered to over 300, including novice through advanced instruction on Microsoft, Novell, Lotus and WordPerfect products. Since 1994, LearnKey has developed numerous interactive CD-ROM tutorials that instruct on the same software topics, which aptly demonstrates LearnKey's ability to stay on the forefront of technology.

Clemons attributes his good fortune and business success to a little luck at being at the right place at the right time with a needed product, great employees and partners, and to his willingness to be patient—rewards always take time.

He has a deep passion for music. As a matter of fact, he says that his main hobby is music. He plays the guitar and sings with a folk group.

How did you choose your profession?

I had an opportunity to get a student job at BYU in video production. I had no skills: I didn't know anything about videos. I made sure that I kept learning things along the way, and that I became more valuable to the crew. I started learning the recording side of the business. From there I went into an editing suite. After the show was shot, it had to be edited. I learned how to run the tape room and editing suite. Late at night I'd go in, put some footage on the tape machines and learn how to edit on my own. One day the editor was sick. They looked at me and said, "Can you really do that?" I said, "Let's give it a try, and if you don't like it, you're not losing anything." Within a few months, I was staff editor. That's the way things worked.

I learned the video business without a formal education; this was accomplished from working and having the initiative to learn on my own. I didn't wait for someone to teach me. That's how I moved through the ranks. Within a very short period of time I was a producer and director for a university. Many college students who were taking the courses were saying, "Why is this guy getting these great opportunities, when we're the ones taking the classes?" It's what you do, not what you learn in a class.

Did you have a family when you started Learn-Key?

Yes, I had a couple of kids. I worked free lance for other video companies, and made good money on the side at night. I was always eager to be a little bit more than just an eight-to-five guy. I'd go work for other people, not only for the money, but for the experience.

We tried some entrepreneurial type things, selling suntan beds, back when that was a hot thing, and selling inflatable swimming pools. We'd go to the trade shows, and the home and garden shows, and try to sell. We got a taste of wanting to be in business for ourselves. Then all of a sudden it just happened. I was able to produce something with the skills I have—a video.

I placed an ad and started selling training videos while I was still working for BYU. It was nothing more than placing an ad, giving somebody an 800 number that I didn't have to answer, and having a post office box.

I had been at BYU for eight years, and felt that I was not going to go a lot further in that job, because the boss took all of the great shows and had me do all of the second level stuff. For a while that's fine, but pretty soon you start to say, "I'm not cut out to be a Hollywood director anyway, so let's go find something else to do."

I wanted to get out on my own, be in business for myself and have some additional freedom. I knew that if I could just sell five tapes a week, that would earn me $1,000 a month; then I would only have to work free lance for other video companies to make $2,000 a month, which was equal to what I was making.

John, was your business an overnight success?

No, we started this business out of the closet. When we started selling the videos, we would go to the post office everyday for three weeks and there would be nothing there; one day we would open the post office box and there would be an order. Somebody gave us money for the videos we produced. Then we would close the post office box and go back the next day to find nothing. Pretty soon, three days later there was another one, and two days later there were two. That's how it started.

Then we figured out that if we could only do five or ten tapes a week, that would not be bad. I did have a partner early in LearnKey. He was a building contractor. I had done some video work for him and he and I had developed a video for a software package that he was using in his construction business. Later we decided to do a video on WordPerfect. I'm the one who did all of the work. I was fortunate enough to buy him out for a very small price.

About a year later I had a very good month. I made more in that month than I had made in a whole year. I recently received a letter from my ex-partner. We had probably not had a conversation for seven years. He is a successful building contractor. In his letter, he said, "I haven't really been watching your company, but all of a sudden I have been seeing several of your magazine ads and thinking about your numbers, 'a million customers in one month.' Congratulations, I'm really proud of you." Receiving that letter was like a pat on the back from my ex-partner. It was one of the highlights of my career.

What are the pros associated with your business?

The definite pros are being able to decide what we want to do on a daily basis. LearnKey has been fortunate to be fairly successful. LearnKey provides us a few extra perks. It allows us to travel. That is a very definite pro.

We get letters from customers, and there have been some interesting comments. People have said, "We loved your product; send us more. It's the best investment we've made." Having satisfied customers says that you are doing something good out there. That does a lot for me. We are very fortunate.

We were one of the first companies to produce the type of videos we make. We made the right product at the right time. We've been very conservative in our spending. Instead of investing in fancy cars or a big salary for me, much of the profit has gone back to the company. My motto is to keep investing in LearnKey.

You own your own plane. Is flying a hobby?

I wouldn't call it a hobby. It became a necessity of the company. We have an office in St. George, Utah, and we have one in Prescott, Arizona. Prescott is on the opposite side of the Grand Canyon from St. George so, it's either an eight hour drive, or an hour and fifteen minute flight. That was part of the incentive.

I happen to live on a hill in St. George, and if I walk a quarter of a mile down the street, I'm at the airport. I would see planes flying in everyday and say, "Gosh I'd love to do that."

How did you train to be a pilot, when did you get your license, and how did the first flight feel?

I bought the plane first—then I had to figure out how to fly it. Since I had bought the plane, I was forced to learn how to fly, and it made me move very fast.

130

At first my wife said, "Don't expect me to get in the plane with you." Then she was ready to get in the plane before she was allowed to. So she started getting a little perturbed that we couldn't use it. She said, "Get your license, I want you to fly me someplace!"

When you're learning to fly, you can't take anybody with you. You have to get your pilot's license first. It took me two months to get my license. It takes most people three or four months. Learning the rules, regulations, and communications takes time, which is really more intimidating than flying the machine. You get over flying the machine within a day or two; it's really not very difficult.

I'm not the greatest pilot in the world. I want to be a good, competent, pilot who follows the rules. I run my business that way, too.

Did you feel fear while flying to California?

Sure I did. Flying to California is a major deal, especially the first time. As a matter of fact, all of my instructors, along with a lot of other people, kept telling me not to fly into California. However, it was a great experience, and I found out that it's not so bad. I landed in Chino; it's not a big airport. You're thick with airports and there's a lot of traffic. We had to fight the haze and the clouds, however, they guided me through it.

Flying is something I wanted to do. I knew I wanted to fly into Phoenix, and that I wanted to be able to fly into California and Las Vegas. I thought at some point I was going to do that, and it would not be a big challenge. It was for my own convenience.

I had to fly into Phoenix; that was a very unnerving thing, however, I found out that it's not that bad, either. I think this is a good example of dealing with fear, rather than avoiding it. At some point you just go and do it.

Do you tend to put things off?

I may put things off, but I don't ignore them. I set priorities. The secret to time management is deciding what's important and then getting rid of that which isn't. A lot of stuff slips through the cracks and doesn't come back to bother you, because it wasn't that important.

I use a day planner and make my *to-do* list. I'm not very effective with it, but I try to keep the important things in front of my face. I do set my priorities, and have my things to do each day, and if I get them done, I feel successful. I'm always looking back over the last two weeks, over the *to-do* list, to see if I've missed anything really important.

You've been very successful. What other companies do you own?

I am successful at starting small companies and being patient to let them grow. We have other companies that have come from LearnKey's success. Three years ago I hired the director of marketing for LearnKey. He had previously been a local advertising executive. In addition to his job at LearnKey, he has built a successful advertising agency under the umbrella of our company. He is seeing his dreams met, and I am building equity in something that will take care of me, as well.

Another company we started over a year ago was an internet provider. Our local community college in St. George was a forerunner in Utah for business on the internet. We collaborated our resources and now have a company that has 400 internet subscribers.

What other businesses have you acquired?

My brother and I have a business in Arizona. He transforms LearnKey video tapes into CD-ROM format. He has an incredible staff; he's a tough manager and they love working for him.

Last but not least, I am one of three owners in a Kawasaki motorcycle dealership. It will be a nice business in three to five years. We've been through two years, and we've gone through some growing pains, but it is a profitable business. It will have its ups and down; it is not a great business to be in—it's a tough business.

You encourage people to go out and do their own thing.

I've hired people whom I think have a lot of capability, and therefore, I'd like to be a part of whatever they're going to do in their life. I'm not going to just exploit them. For instance, we have a young man who has extremely good electronic skills. He could probably figure out how to build a radio and other small electrical devices. We have some ideas that he's slowly working on. Hopefully, one day he'll create a device that we can market.

Is there anyone in your life who makes you feel like a success?

Well, certainly my wife does. She's my biggest fan and we're great friends. There's nobody that I'd rather go to lunch with than my wife. We enjoy conversation. She used to be involved in the business on a part-time basis when it was a *mom and pop* thing, until a year ago.

She did some of the bookkeeping. She's always been understanding in what we do and involved to a certain degree. Now she spends more time with the children.

133

We met at college. We were actually good friends for a year, but hadn't dated. In fact, she dated everybody but me. Then suddenly we looked at each other and said we ought to date. We dated for a year, and then we married. We love to do things as a family. Travel is probably our biggest interest.

How do your children respond to your busy life-style?

I think they enjoy it, and they get to travel. I tend to be available for most of their things. If I need to be there, I'm there. Business doesn't interfere that much with our life. I don't do a lot of business travel and I don't work a lot of late nights. I'd say that there's a pretty good balance between my family and my work.

Have you ever felt like a failure?

No, I think my folks were good at trying to make me a leader. In high school I always seemed to pick a position on a team. On the football team, I was the quarterback, and on the baseball team I was a catcher. In college I was involved in student government. I've never considered myself a failure.

How do you prevent failure?

I don't bite off more than I can chew. I have patience and work slow. I don't expect the world right away. When we went into the motorcycle business, the two main partners said, "Do not expect anything out of this business for five to ten years." It's the same thing with the advertising agency, and the internet provider. That's not a huge long-term goal, but three to five years in a business is pretty long-term. It means putting revenues back in, investing and letting the companies grow.

How do you ensure that you don't get cheated?

Every time I've gone into business, I've said that I will control the money. For a while I signed all of the checks. The motorcycle dealership with two principals that are outside the business are the only two who can sign the checks. I only pick those whom I can trust. I have great people working with me. It's the same thing in the advertising agency.

How did you know you were going to be successful?

I have an inner belief that I can do things. I'm really a good jack-of-all-trades, so whether it's fixing the toilet, running the business, or placing an ad, I'm pretty good at most things. I have belief in myself that I can do just about anything. I'm not a rocket scientist, I'm not doing nuclear things, but those things that I am doing, I'm pretty good at. In my personal life, I'm working to become a better parent. In the music area, I'm working to become a better performer.

Are you good at giving control to others?

Yes, and no. I've tried to give control to others, and in some cases it has worked out really well. I am probably still the one with the most experience in creating video programs. That's my background. The people that we have hired have been trained by me.

Since they haven't really experienced video production for other clients and with other individuals, I tend to keep going back in there, making suggestions, and feeling as if I need to be involved in the actual video production. That has changed.

We just hired one other person in the last year who has pretty good experience. I do not tend to hire any experienced individuals in LearnKey, with rare exception. Generally we bring them in because of their personality and show them what we're doing.

Does training take a lot of your time?

Sometimes it does. But sometimes I get a surprise, too. I see things on my desk and say, "Wow, that's better than what I could have done. Thank you!" Often when errors show up, I say, "If I could have spent a little more time with those guys, I could have fixed some of the obvious problems." I'm not a high-end video producer, but there are certain 101 rules that you don't break, or certain things that might have made it a little nicer.

Do you allow others to assign value or self-worth to you?

I think I have a grasp on who I am, and I have a good grasp on where I fit. I don't think of myself too highly, nor do I think of myself too lowly. I think I'm pretty good at certain things, really average in most things, and I've gotten fortunate somewhere along the line because of a little bit of drive. What other people say about me doesn't really matter—good or bad.

What makes you accept advice from people?

I'm generally looking behind the scenes...what do these people really want? I tend to be pretty critical about where the message is coming from, what the advice is, and what's in it for the other person. It can be good, but I do want to know what's in it for the advice giver, so I can make a good decision for LearnKey.

When I accept your advice I tend to want to move real slow and take a little time on all decisions I make. I tend to come up with the best answers, comebacks, or decisions three to four days later.

When do you feel good about yourself?

I feel good about myself most of the time. I feel good about myself when I do something nice for somebody else. For my employees, I feel really good when there's a surprise bonus. When my family and I go to a rest home and do a little musical performance, we walk away feeling pretty good, and we think, "Gosh, we have to do more of that kind of thing."

We have a local concert series in St. George that I'm involved in. I put up sound and that makes me feel good. We are a small group that coordinates concerts. I bring in outside performers to put on a free concert series. That's my voluntary effort, although it has turned into my hobby, something that I love a lot. It feels really neat when the concert comes off successfully. I spend a lot of time with this concert series. I feel good, because I'm giving something to the community.

When do you feel bad about yourself?

I guess when I start getting paranoid and nervous about the business, it shows on my face. Everybody reads me. I'm home five seconds and my wife knows what kind of day I've had and my employees do, too. I'm pretty focused on what I'm doing, but they can see when I'm a little stressed. I'm not a real bubbly, uplifting, motivational leader most of the time; I get a little nervous, and a little down with the constant challenges that we have, so that's when I'm feeling the worse.

Looking back on your career, do you have any regrets?

Yes, I'm wondering why I didn't do it three years earlier. In fact, that's what I tell most people. It's hard to come in and buy a half-million dollar business, and be successful. It's not hard to be successful with a business out of the closet.

Overcoming Doubt, Fear and Procrastination

***What advice do you have for overcoming doubt,
fear and procrastination?***

The main advice I would give is to embrace change. I would look for change almost every time. Change is good. Bringing in different people into the business is good. It shakes things up. Different people bring different ideas. If you want to do better, you have to change. Another key to success is the initiative. Just do it. Try it. Try it small enough that it doesn't kill you. Those are things I live by.

9) Overcoming The Obstacles— The Real Story

Successful individuals are not exempt from doubt, fear and procrastination, they just respond to them differently.

It's not everyday that we're invited into the private lives of successful individuals. We can't help but wonder, what is the real glue that holds them together? How do they rise above life's major frustrations and minor aggravations? Is there a deep, dark secret known only to those who have achieved success?

The truth is, successful individuals are not exempt from hurt, pain and disappointment. The road to success has many crooks and turns, each yielding the tenacious traveler different results. You may experience enormous joy one day and mind-boggling disappointment the next. One thing is for certain, you will come to realize that part of the arrival is being in the moment, and learning to meet adversity head-on, by strapping on your boots and rolling up your sleeves.

The successful traveler remains focused, keeping his or her eye on the prize—never faltering—never wavering, taking only a momentary pause to regroup. These road warriors possess the knowledge and skills needed to evaluate and enjoy the journey to success.

Overcoming Doubt, Fear and Procrastination

These individuals have reached success spanning from all walks of life and all levels of financial and economic independence. But there is one thing they all have in common: They have the ability to understand the true meaning of success. They have defined success for themselves, and on their own terms. They maintain a spirit of self-confidence and self-esteem that is apparent from the moment you meet them.

These courageous travelers have elected not to give in to doubt, fear and procrastination. They have chosen to move beyond their comfort zone and embrace change. Through their valiant efforts, these road warriors remained on course even when change seemed to bear less than desirable fruit. They remained on course in the midst of criticism, when others around them questioned their judgment. For all of their hard work and determination, the journey yielded their true reward—success.

As we turn the pages, we are given carte blanche to invade the privacy of Americana's successful elite, as they share with us the glue that held them together to triumph over doubt, fear and procrastination.

Jane Myers Drew, PhD

Jane Myers Drew, PhD, is a psychologist in private practice in Newport Beach, California. She approaches her work with a willingness to be open and teachable. She has a rich life experience from which she draws, in order to touch her clients with care and compassion.

Dr. Drew was the youngest of five children in Racine, Wisconsin. Her father died when she was fourteen months old, and she was raised by a powerful and domineering mother. She spent most of her youth attempting to measure up to her mother's expectations.

Her early life experiences became the catalyst for her dynamic work in the area of healing emotional wounds.

Dr. Drew is the author of two books: *Where Were You When I Needed You Dad?: A Guide For Healing Your Father Wound,* and *Show Me How To Love You: Creating Your Own Couples Support Group,* which is forthcoming in the fall of 1996. In addition, she is a

141

speaker and workshop facilitator who travels throughout the US training other professionals in her work. Her hobbies are sports, singing and painting.

Dr. Jane Myers Drew shares her thoughts on fear:

Fear...those things that scare me when there is a conflict of whether to hold back or go forward. This is a natural human occurrence—we all have fears. I don't want to make this bad or pathological, because everyone has these and in deep layers: Fear of inadequacy, of being rejected, or of being abandoned, to name a few. It seems to me, the real power is getting in touch with the fact that the fears are there, and then saying: "Okay, I see my fears, and I can move forward." The thing that blocks people is that they are not willing to look inside; they are reacting and thinking: "I should do this," and then they go charging off without feeling integrated from the inside out.

I feel that procrastination is closely connected with fear. As I work with my clients, I see the ones who don't try things. They feel that if they put in all that effort and try things, it won't get them anywhere. It has a lot to do with their belief systems. A lot of people were exposed to belief systems from their parents that were not empowering.

We have natural inclinations as to how hard we want to work or how high we want to reach, and I think it is important to tune in to those feelings. We are not all meant to be doing the same thing and to be highly successful in the world's terms. I believe we are pre-programmed to do what is right for us. We know by tuning in to our intuition. Success doesn't have to be working twelve hour days and making lots of money.

Are the symptoms relating to doubt, fear and procrastination physiological or psychological?

My symptoms are mostly physiological. For example, during my TV appearances, sometimes my throat closes down, and my hands get cold. What I do to overcome the symptoms is a kind of meditation where I sit down, breath deeply and talk to myself. *You are here, you are going to do it. Most of life is showing up and you are going to do the best you can. If you make a mistake, I will still love you.*

Self-talk is very helpful. It is similar to what you would do with a small child. You wouldn't be mad at him. You would sit down next to him, put your arm around him and say, "I am here, it's okay, you're okay. We'll get through this."

Can therapy help?

For me, I think going into therapy made a big difference. I had someone who really cared and listened without judgment. There were things that I had never shared with anyone, because I didn't believe that a person could listen and not think that I was terrible. I was busy hiding myself and trying to look successful.

What I now understand is that I need to belong to a group that I can be with every week. It doesn't have to be a therapy group. I had a long-term women's group in my life. It was just a group of us where we would get together and share with each other. We shared our thoughts, challenges and circumstances, such as, "This is what I am dealing with in my life....This is what I am feeling....This is what's going on....," and we showed each other that we cared.

When do you find yourself putting things off, and how do you justify doing so?

I put things off when I'm afraid I don't know how to do something, when I think it's going to be more work than I want to do, or when I'm afraid the outcome won't be what I want. I then tell myself that it would be better to do it next week, to give it a little more time, or to see if it resolves itself on its own. I may tell myself that I've been working too hard, so I'll just not do this now.

Do you feel that you have achieved a level of success?

I have been successful at having a wonderful practice where I am really helping people. I was successful in getting my PhD, writing, publishing and promoting my book. I figure I have reached eighteen million people. I have had articles in *USA Today, LA Times,* and the *New York Daily News.* I have appeared on the *Home Show,* have been featured in about five TV programs, and have been on approximately forty radio talk shows.

Are you successful in personal relationships?

I grew up in a family where there was a lot of blaming. It was always the other person's fault. I have learned not to pass the blame. However, I do make the other people aware of what my feelings are and why I am feeling that way. They may have said something that hurt me. I am not blaming them for saying it, I am telling them what happened inside of me that caused me to have hurt feelings.

Years of therapy have helped. Now, I can look into relationships and see that there are two major modes to them. One way is to protect myself and feel defensive, and the other way is to go beneath the protection and defenses and be open to learn about myself and to learn about my partner.

I catch myself now when I am defensive. I realize that I have a choice. I know all the ways I can be defensive: a little silent treatment; punishing the other person; blaming; withdrawing; trying to please him; indifference (I don't care, do whatever you want—it matters not to me). Now I don't have to get what I want. I can understand the other person, and figure out what's going on with me.

Have you ever felt like a failure?

I have felt like a failure many times. A lot of it had to do with my own expectations or definition of what success is, especially at an early time in my life; whatever I had done was just not good enough. Success was just beyond what I had done. I have learned to appreciate what I have done, and to let that be justifying. That makes me more willing to do other things.

What do you think causes people to fail?

What I see most is that people don't even try. They have decided in their minds that while they like something, they can't do it. It's just too much work, and it wouldn't work anyway. Before they even start, they condemn themselves. They want to be something, but rather than sacrifice and do whatever it may take to become what they want to be, they settle for something easier, but less rewarding.

Do you have a strong belief in yourself and your abilities?

I've been around long enough to know that I have been successful in both my personal life and my professional life. I have paid my dues, and I have learned a lot. While writing my first book, everything loomed at me like a nine-foot wall: How do you do a copyright? How do you do a book proposal? How do you do this, and so on? The second book will be easier to get published, because I know how to do all those things. It was hard, it was a challenge. It was like learning to ski; the first day out on the slopes I wanted to quit, but I stuck with it, and now I love to ski. The first time or the beginning of anything, we have to pay our dues. Unfortunately, we feel humiliated if we don't get it right away.

Are you good at giving control to others?

I am good at giving control to others when it is theirs. I want to keep the control that's mine. I am good at giving control as long as I can see that they can do the job. I give it to them, and have them report back, but I am not hovering over them.

One of the reasons I self-published my book is because I didn't want to give control to a publisher. I didn't know what the publisher would do with it. But for this next book, I learned that keeping control was too much work, so now I'm willing to give up that control. I didn't see it like that at one time. I just thought that to insure the success of my book, I needed to do it, and maintain all of the control. Now I see that I can join with other people who have more experience and more expertise; by working together with them, maybe I can even do better. I am learning all the time.

Do you allow others to assign value or self-worth to you?

Yes and no. The *no* part is that I know it has to come from me. I also know that when we have people close to us, how they feel about us does affect us. Having good relationships is important; but it's not so much who you pick that is important, but it is how you relate to each other. *I used to think it was who I picked that* was important. Now I am realizing that how I treat the person has much more to do with how good the relationship is!

What makes you accept or disregard advice from others?

If the person giving the advice is an expert on the topic being discussed, I would be more likely to listen. Often I will feel out several people for advice and see which one feels the best to me; or maybe it's the advice I am the most willing to follow. Sometimes I try to take my own counsel; but I am certainly open for advice, because there is a lot that people have to offer me.

Does the opinion of others weigh heavily on your mind?

No, if I have put a lot of work and heart into a project, nothing is going to stop me. I use my inner guidance. People have a lot of advice out there. When it is a positive opinion, it certainly gives me a boost. When it is a negative opinion, it is like a little pinprick. It influences me, but in the end I ask myself, "What is my mission? What is my purpose for being here on this earth?" That's the biggest issue for me.

Do you need the approval or acceptance of a loved one in order to proceed with your goals?

It certainly helps, but it's not necessary. This is my life's work, and sometimes my family doesn't understand what I want, or why I want to do this, or why I keep pushing myself. Over the years I have become my own individual.

Do you see yourself as a perfectionist?

There is no doing it perfectly. I am not a perfectionist, however, I do have high standards. I don't have a perfectionism that paralyzes me.

What is your definition of denial?

To me, denial is when I am not seeing something for what it is. Denial is when I am pretending. It is as if I am pushing something away, not looking at it, and saying, "Oh, everything is okay." I'm not really letting myself see what's going on.

When do you feel good about yourself?

I especially feel good about myself when I have some wins. I feel good about myself when I'm working on my book. When I'm working on something that is hard and it's coming together, then I feel great! I feel great when I take a weekend off, go camping and have fun.

I feel good about myself in the couples' group when I am being open, vulnerable and working on things, helping others to work on things, and being close. I can show the darkest part of myself and know that I am still loved and cared about. It's what we have all set up together, this really non-judgmental thing. There is support for each person, because from our point of view, we all have good reasons for what we do. If someone can tap into my good reasons, I feel more understood, and I am more likely to shift. *Oh, I see now.* It's an incredible atmosphere of acceptance and caring.

Are there times when you feel bad about yourself?

I feel bad about myself if I work too much and start to feel depleted. It could even be a small thing, such as, paperwork coming back and I have to redo it. Or, if something that I've hoped comes through doesn't; then I start to feel down or discouraged. Dr. John Gray, who wrote *Men are from Mars, Women are from Venus,* says that women are like a wave. Emotionally they go up and down. I have become more tolerant of my little ups and downs. I don't get so freaked out when I have days when I don't have as much energy and I don't get as much done.

I believe that you must go deep within yourself and ask a number of questions so you can learn what's going on with you: *Why am I feeling bad? Is there something I want to do that I am not doing? Is there some belief about myself that is causing me to act a certain way?*

For example, you have a desire and are frustrated from not acting on it because of someone else. You finally act on your desire, and you feel good because that's what you wanted all along. There is a good book that addresses this issue called, *Do I Have to Give Up Me to be Loved by You?*, by Jordan and Margaret Paul.

Do you have any fears?

I have feelings of fear if I am giving a new presentation or workshop: Am I going to be accepted? Have I done a good job? Will I be rejected? These are universal fears that we all have to some extent.

I have some lurking fears that keep showing up in my life differently. They are not so big as they used to be: Will I be alone? Will I have friends? There were times in my life when I would spend lots of time alone, I was isolated. When being alone is out of choice—I like it.

How do you plan to overcome your fears?

I plan to keep being aware that they are there, rather than pushing them away. I am a planner, and I try to make things happen in my life. If I should find myself without friends or a support group, I know that there are things I can do. I can start a women's group. I can ask women in. I can find that support. I can find other groups I can belong to and know I can meet people there.

Please share what this statement mean to you: Determination equals success!

The first thing I think of is, "Where does the determination come from? Does your desire to accomplish a goal just show up?" I am interested in finding out what motivates me and other people, knowing what is important, and how important is that achievement? How determined are you to put out effort to reach your dreams?

For those people who are having a hard time believing, if you deeply want something for a good reason, God is going to help you find a way to have it happen, if it is within His will. For instance, I don't want to be an opera singer, so I don't spend energy on that, but there are things I want to do that are meaningful to me, so I will combine prayer and determination, which includes hard work, to make those ideals become a reality.

Let's say that I want to be a ballerina. At my age that's probably not going to happen. But, if I keep having the desire, maybe I should get myself into a class to fulfill my need, not on a grand scale, such as being sixteen and wanting to be in a ballerina company, but on a realistic, reachable scale that would be fun and beneficial for my body.

You have mentioned God and faith. Do you believe in a higher spiritual power?

I definitely believe in a higher power and that there is a specific place for me. I ask for guidance. I try to open my inner being to be moved. I wake up every morning, and my first thoughts are to be grateful for what I have and to ask for guidance during the day.

I'll be doing a session, and I'll really want to help the person or people, but I won't know quite what to say. I'll pray to the Lord, "Please make me a channel; help to fill me with your strength and wisdom, and please give me your guidance."

What advice do you have for overcoming doubt, fear, and procrastination?

What I'd like people to do is to be able to hold all the parts of themselves, as if they were holding them in front of them. And, to know that everyone is a mixture of some really good attributes and some difficult ones. Because we each have a dark side, we have some fears and some doubts, and that's okay. It is just a part of who we are; it doesn't have to stop us. We can get support from other people, and we can began to appreciate how magnificent we are, and how much there is to be grateful for. As we begin to focus on all the good things in our lives, the difficult things will come into balance and not overwhelm us.

Here is a cute little story: *There was a man who wrote a poem a day, and someone asked him, "How do you possibly write a poem a day?" He said, "I lower my standards."* Setting and attaining realistic goals builds one's confidence.

Cecil Whiting, PhD

Dr. Cecil C. Whiting was born and raised in the central area of Cleveland, Ohio. He attended Central State University in Wilberforce, Ohio, and graduated in 1966 with a bachelor of science degree in music education. He became the band director of Cleveland John Hay High School from 1966 to 1969.

While teaching in Cleveland Schools, Dr. Whiting became one of the founders of the Cleveland Association of Black Educators and a founder of the Black Information Service. During the evenings and summers, he attended graduate school and majored in educational psychology at John Carroll University until 1971.

In 1971, he entered the graduate program of the combined program in education and psychology at the University of Michigan, where he earned a master's degree in 1973 and a doctor of philosophy degree in education and psychology in 1974. After graduation, Dr. Whiting took a position as an assistant director of the

Community Mental Health Center at Meharry Medical College in Nashville, Tennessee. In 1975 he became co-ordinator of adult, outpatient services at Kedren Community Mental Health Center in Los Angeles and in 1980, Dr. Whiting became director of children's services at Central City Mental Health Center.

Since 1981, Dr. Whiting has been a psychologist in private practice in the Los Angeles area. He has taught the *Psychology of the African American* in the department of Afro-ethnic studies at California State University at Fullerton since 1988.

Dr. Whiting has written articles for the *Mothering Section* of *Essence Magazine* on *Gifted Black Children*, the *Advocate* for the Los Angeles County Bar Association and *The Case of the Spiked Brain* in *For the Defense*. He has written one novel entitled, *Tales of Tichuba* and a large non-fiction treatise on the psychology of Africans entitled, *Blacklash*.

Dr. Whiting, how do you define procrastination?

I define procrastination pretty much the same way I describe avoidance; not letting something that would cause you fear to occur; being somewhere else—doing something else—distracting yourself.

In most cases it is not just laziness; procrastination is more of an organizational flaw, when people have allowed something or some aspect of fear to impose on them. I say that reluctantly, because it could be something as complex as success.

It is important for people to recall experiences when they have been successful; this will encourage them to move past procrastination and on to do something constructive. For me it is essential, if I am doing something and am struggling with it. For example, I often remind myself that I have done it before—I can do this! Basically, what I am doing is giving myself verbal reinforcement. Anything you tell yourself that is affirming is important, because it keeps you going.

How much value should be placed on another person's opinion?

If you are doing something that's going to be highly criticized, and you understand that criticism first, then you are able to cope with the criticism when it comes. The opinion of others shouldn't weigh so heavily that it becomes incapacitating. If someone is saying something that is less than supportive about your efforts, you have to examine it, because there might be some validity. You should examine it to see if it applies to you and if it can be used to help. It might be a biting criticism, but you have to accept it, based upon the idea that within a biting criticism there may be something constructive.

You do not need someone to validate your work; simply knowing that you are doing a good job should be validation enough. After you have had enough experience and developed your own expertise, you can be confident. At that point what other people say doesn't result in either defensiveness or any diminishing of self-worth. For example, someone could tell me that I am a lousy psychologist; I would be sufficiently non-defensive and ask, "What makes you say that?"

Are you afraid of success?

Success is defined as the functional autonomy of motives. For example, my life's goal was to become a really good and well-known jazz musician. However, I am not doing that. It doesn't mean that I am not successful; it means that I am not doing everything I originally planned to do and I have not pursued that particular goal.

A functional autonomous motive is a motive that drives you toward a goal that might change in the future through association. To give another example, as an undergraduate I majored in music. To be able to play music I needed to get an income; I became a music teacher. Instead of getting a straight music degree, I got a bachelor of science in music with an emphasis in education.

After teaching music, I found that there were a lot of other needs within the school system. I had a number of students who had difficulties, so I went into guidance counseling. I enrolled into the university with the idea of going into guidance counseling, but the program was closed and the only course that was open was educational psychology. I was told that I could transfer the credits to guidance later on, so I began a major in educational psychology.

As I became more interested, I decided that psychology might be more in line with what I wanted to do to help the kids that were in my band and orchestra. At that point, my motives had become functionally autonomous. I hadn't lost sight of my original goal, because somewhere in the back of my mind was still a jazz musician. To this day, I have my trumpet and I still practice, but I am currently not moving in the direction of my original goal.

I think that I have been successful in achieving goals all along. Some people refer to success as being lucky; luck is when preparation meets opportunity. There are a combination of elements that equal success: Ability, preparation, and opportunity. That's what success is, and it changes as the person grows.

Success when you are twenty years old might be getting a car. Success when you are thirty might be having a happy home and family; when you're forty it might be having a fulfilling career, and at fifty it might be having a good retirement plan.

Can success alienate a person from a reference group?

One of our societal problems is that we equate success with the accumulation of money. That is not necessarily a good measure of success. Some individuals have problems with success when it changes their reference group. Their interaction with others is hampered, and success separates them from their reference group.

If you are dealing with people who are used to specific interpersonal interactions, and you take them away from those interactions, they can become fearful. They do not become fearful of success itself, but what success denotes. To them, it may mean separation, withdrawal, and perhaps even alienation from a reference group. The most effective way to involve these individuals in successful issues is to do so as a group. If the group is successful, then the individuals will be successful. However, if they have to leave the group individually to become successful, the individual success may mean that they can't go back to their group. They've grown beyond that group, and that can be painful.

Industry has a different mission. The industries and institutions that influence our lives give us the criteria for success. The real criteria for success on an individual basis has to be personalized. If you have accepted someone else's perception or definition of success for yourself, then you are destined to become successful according to that person's definition, rather than to your own definition of success.

Are there specific character traits that are indicative of successful people?

It is important to realize that the thoughts and actions of creative, successful people will not always be consistent with what you might expect in the majority of the population. Successful people tend to think differently.

There have been some studies conducted using the Minnesota Multiphasic Personality Inventory, which is probably the most widely used psychological test. It has been given to creative people, such as artists. Those people come out high on the schizophrenia scale, which may mean that you have to be a little bit crazy in order to be creative. However, you can only be a little bit crazy, because if you are too crazy, then the craziness takes over.

In a creative sense, compulsiveness doesn't hurt. Compulsive people are those who get up in the morning and know where their keys are, the special pen that they are going to write with, and where their wallet is. If one of those items is missing, they may be late for work because they can't find it. That is compulsivity. That's an energizer of success, even though it seems as though it delays people. When you think of someone being late by having his agenda turned upside-down due to little things, that person is being sufficiently compulsive. People who exhibit this type of behavior will have sufficient follow-through and tenacity on the major projects so the tasks will be done efficiently. Being compulsive in this sense is not bad.

Now we have a semi-schizophrenic and compulsive person. We also want to have just a touch of anxiety—butterfies in the stomach, a little nervousness, a little bit of pride about the production of whatever it is that he or she is doing. When a person has schizophrenic compulsiveness and is suffering from a little bit of anxiety, that person is probably going to be more successful than someone who doesn't care. The "don't care" person is someone who goes along with the program and has no real compulsion to achieve something.

What are some causes of failure?

Some people tend to be overly impulsive and vacillate from pillar to post. There are people who are too conventional—that's the opposite side of schizophrenia. These people want to do things the right way—*just tell me how to do it—tell me how it's supposed to go—I need to follow the instructions.*

People who put things together without the instructions will probably be more successful than people who have to rely on instructions. There are roles for people who put things together by the instructions, but being creative is not one of them.

A person who is overly calm and doesn't get nervous may not be too successful. You have to be a little bit spacy from my perspective, a little bit unconventional, and you have to have enough passion in what you are doing so that the possibility of failure makes you nervous.

Roberta Pierce

Roberta Pierce, vice-president of sales and operations for a fast growing, Southern California based temporary employment service, is a successful business executive with a passion for what she does. Her 20 years of business experience has been a unique blend of the structured corporate climate, as well as the wonderful entrepreneurial environment. The company she directs is responsible for putting thousands of people to work each year. She finds her career incredibly satisfying and says part of her tremendous motivation comes from seeing the growth of those members of her staff, as well as her passion for successful, healthy teamwork. She is a business executive who sincerely believes that people are our greatest asset.

Roberta is a dedicated wife, mother, and grandmother. She believes with great confidence that people can do whatever they desire, if they are truly willing to apply themselves to the cause and commit 100% without wavering. Roberta has learned success is all about

159

accountability and responsibility. There is no time for doubt, fear and procrastination.

Have you ever experienced doubt, fear and procrastination?

Yes, I have. I honestly think that I grew up as a child with all of those. I grew up in a family that did not believe in taking risks, in order to avoid failure and losing what you had. I grew up believing that. As I got older, I would try little things and break through some of those barriers. I started experiencing success in small areas that made me feel very satisfied and made me think, "Wow, if I can do that, what if I tried this?" One little stepping-stone led to another. Over a period of 25-30 years, I have gone from being afraid to try anything that involves risks to getting to the point where I always look for an opportunity. It has been a long process. I try to discipline myself whenever I realize that I am worrying. I remind myself that concern is fine, worry is not.

Can you recall when you understood the power of discipline in your life?

Actually, it was about eight years ago when I really got a handle on it. I was working for a company, and was in a personal situation that was disastrous. My husband's business failed, he had health problems, and everything came crashing down on us. Then I realized that I had a job where the harder I worked, the more I broke barriers, the more I got out of my comfort zone, and the greater the return on my investment and time. I could have gone the other way, and said, "Oh, I'm so overcome with worry, because I don't know how we're going to pay these bills. And I'm not sure how my husband's health is going to be." That is really where I learned to discipline myself and say, "You know what, it's one day at a time, and I'm going to tackle this thing eight hours at a time. I'm going to move out here, because this is my road to success. I can sit here and be worried and fearful, and procrastinate, and go down the tubes, or I can take the opportunity and go for it, big time."

Do you tend to put things off?

There are things that I put off, but I don't put off the things that are vital. There are certain things that I know I can't put off. In business, when it comes to the people who work for me, I don't procrastinate. I stop what I am doing to help them. When I feel things are getting away from me, I immediately make a list. Then I make sure I get it all checked off, clear my slate, and move forward.

What has brought you success?

I think that my number one success, absolutely, has been in being a mother. That's my greatest success in life; it is being a mother to two beautiful people who are now adults and have children of their own.

I can recall, going back to when they were babies, and when they were little girls, I was going through a divorce. I was sad about them not having a father. I made a commitment to my children that I would do whatever I had to do, to be mom and dad, and I would do everything to the best of my ability.

Now I can look back and say, "What a joy." Being a mother is my biggest success, without question.

Is there anyone in your life who makes you feel like a success?

I wouldn't say there is one person who makes me feel successful. My family is very supportive. Whether or not you have someone praising you, you

161

owe it to yourself to do a good job. We need to support ourselves. We need to recognize what success means to us, and just seize the opportunity.

Have you ever felt like a failure?

When I went through my divorce, I felt like a failure. I think that is pretty typical. When people go through a divorce, they tend to blame themselves and wonder, "If I had done this, or if I had done that...." I got over that feeling, because I realized that I can't beat myself up for it; it just didn't work. So I moved on, made the best of everything, and tried to learn from the situation.

How did you overcome the feeling?

I was 25 years old when I was going through my divorce, and honestly and truly, I had never heard the term, *self-esteem*. Isn't that amazing? I got a hold of a couple of books on self-esteem. What I realized was, there is a word called self-esteem, and I learned how it impacts your life and your direction. I was going through hard times, and I needed some direction. I needed to feel better about myself. I was hungry for this stuff; I just couldn't get enough books. That's when I started growing up. That's when I realized that I might be young, I might have two small children, and I might not be making a lot of money right now, but I made this full-blown commitment to these two kids, that I will give them my best. I better get myself in gear, quit feeling sorry for myself and get busy.

I believe 100 percent in myself. I might find myself in a situation that is displeasing to me. I'm not going to let it alter my destiny. I have found myself in situations when it was time to move on. And when I felt it was time to move on, that's what I did. The good news is, when you move on with that kind of an attitude, new things start falling your way, or you start focusing on some new adventures, and you're back on track.

I learned several years ago that I can't let anything negative affect me. If I am having a hard time with something at home, with something personal, when I leave home, I leave it there, literally. When I come back home, if I need to pick up baggage and deal with it, then I will. But I'm not going to let a problem there create a problem that inundates my whole life. I am committed to keeping my personal life and my business life separate. Balance is the key to a successful life.

How did you become an effective manager?

I think my biggest ground work for becoming an effective manager goes back to being the mother of two girls who were very assertive and aggressive, and only 18 months apart. I was always concerned with fairness and tried to instill values in them. It kept me aware, moment by moment, and day by day, of what was happening, and it helped me to look at things from a different perspective. How does it make them feel if I make this decision? How does it make that person feel if I present it this way? A lot of those same principles apply at work. When I work with people, I make a real commitment to them, and I want them to be successful. I buy into their success; it goes back to that same relationship with my daughters. I want them to be a success, and I want to do all the right things. I just adore the people who are committed to me, and I am committed to them. I try to always keep that balance, and they know that.

What about the praise factor?

I like to praise people. And I like the old principle, _praise in public, but criticize in private._ Not that I like to criticize, but sometimes people need to be re-minded of things, or they need to be told that's not quite how to do it. I try to make sure that I operate by that principle. I have learned that you should never bring conflict to an open forum. You deal with conflict one-on-one. You share all the wonderful things in an open forum. But a conflict is a personal thing, and it needs to be handled that way.

It is important to have everyone on your team 100 percent behind you. If I feel I have someone on my team who is questionable, I feel a tremendous need to sit down with that person and say, "Let's talk. I'm not feeling right about this. Something's not there. Let's talk about our commitment level. Is there something going on?" It will usually turn around. I had a person who worked for me. She was very good at what she did; I just didn't feel a sense of loyalty after a while. We sat down to talk and I said, "Let me tell you how I work. I am committed, 110 percent, lock, stock, and barrel, to your success; but do you know what I need back in re-turn? I need that same commitment from you." I am happy to say that in the last two years, knock on wood, I have had not one person quit.

When do you accept advice from people?

I am very open to accepting advice from other people. I really like hearing other people's perspectives and hearing what worked for them. I like people to feel empowered. I like people to make decisions and like to surround myself with assertive people. I feel that's how you really maximize your effectiveness. If someone's try-ing to give me advice, and it is somebody who doesn't even take his or her own advice, then it is not worth much to me. I believe that you need to be somewhat cautious about from whom you receive advice.

Are you a perfectionist?

There are things that are real important to me and they need to be done correctly. I'm a perfectionist in the sense that everything has to feel right to me. If it feels right, then I'm fine. I'm not going to let something go out that I can find an error in. I don't get real hung up on feeling that everything has to be perfect, because if I did, we would never get anything done. If each one of my staff is giving a hundred percent, then I'm okay. I can't be running around behind each one of them saying, "Uh-oh, you forgot this," or "You didn't cross this _t_" because I'd be nuts.

What advice do you have in closing?

Why hold yourself back because you are doubtful, or because you are fearful? It is not necessarily the smartest man who becomes successful, but it is the one who is the most committed. If you are committed to your own success, just start dealing with the obstacles and begin plowing through them.

S. Barry Hamdani

S. Barry Hamdani began his business career immediately upon graduating from California State University at Los Angeles, where he earned a bachelor's degree in business.

Barry has since founded and sold two successful enterprises. In the summer of 1980, he founded the Entrepreneurs Club of Los Angeles (ECLA), which consisted of a series of newsletters geared toward a variety of business disciplines, i.e., sales and marketing finance, etc. The company was sold in 1985 at a very handsome profit to Barry. He later created a national magazine which was introduced to the market in June of 1990. The publication was read by college students and generated revenue mainly through full-page advertisement placement from corporate recruiters. In 1994, the title was sold to a publishing conglomerate.

Barry has since established SBH Professional Services, Inc., an exclusive line of custom clothing for men. His designs have already become a staple in the

Atlanta market. Among an impressive client base are former mayor Maynard Jackson, the Honorable Ural Glanville, the Honorable William C. Randall, Senator Ralph David Abernathy III, Ed Turner, Les Brown, Clarence Beard (publisher of the Black Business Journal), a host of doctors and attorneys, and many industry leaders including presidents of colleges and universities, and sports personalities. Barry is flown around the country to fit clients, review wardrobes, and assess additions to new product lines by major designers and merchandisers. He is currently reviewing a new line of shirts for Ralph Lauren under the Polo label in conjunction with Mike Allman, President of the Bibb Company.

Barry's company will soon introduce a men's custom clothing catalog featuring his latest designs (the first catalog of its kind).

Barry and his lovely wife, Arlys, reside in Stone Mountain, a suburb of Metro Atlanta. They enjoy tennis, golf, and an occasional stroll through the historical Stone Mountain Park.

Their message to the readers of *Overcoming Doubt, Fear, and Procrastination* is to "put the study into practice by believing in something greater than oneself....elevate to the higher calling."

What is your definition of fear?

Each time I find myself fearful to the slightest degree, I ask myself why I am feeling this way. More often than not, the entity or circumstances I fear are those which are least likely to happen. Therefore, in my experience, fear is a state of mind. It does not require reason and is generally unfounded and not supported by my better intelligence.

Overcoming Doubt, Fear and Procrastination

What is your definition of procrastination?

If I fail to prepare for a given task, or if I fail to analyze whatever reservations I have regarding a given task, I will automatically procrastinate. Consequently, I must conclude that procrastination is poor time management regarding one's important affairs. It is a sibling of the unfocused.

For instance, I recently found myself crowded and overwhelmed with responsibilities, projects, deadlines and additional emerging interest. As a result, I failed to complete most of my projects on time. Therefore, I took a short trip to a new environment alone.

When I returned, I felt rejuvenated and focused. I knew exactly what I wanted to complete, postpone, eliminate and plan. I completed my projects in record time and worried about none of them.

Have you ever experienced doubt, fear and procrastination?

Yes. Because I am actively creating and experimenting with my business interest, I feel a presence of each of these monsters for a moment each day, but I've learned to run them away by referring to my goals and past accomplishments, and by referring to my time as an investment.

Each investment will not generate a good return, but if I continue to invest in a few projects, just moments each day, my overall portfolio of time will offer a great return. This attitude destroys procrastination, which is dependent upon it's partners, fear and doubt.

Are you always aware of the symptoms that cause doubt, fear and procrastination?

No. Only in retrospect will I see them clearly. However, I write down all of my plans and goals—business and personal, and if I am not doing something each

168

day to meet them, this chart will act as a gauge, alerting me that something is wrong. I then pray, or use whatever spiritual exercise necessary to bring these problems to the forefront. This never fails for me. My truth is soon manifested. I then refer to books and notes that I have used before. These notes are like a doctor's prescription. I use them to overcome an illness and to restore my state of mind. The spiritual exercise diagnoses me at a higher level and makes my symptoms manifest. My notes are my prescription. All I need to do is to read and apply what I have read.

Do you tend to put things off?

Yes. If I have not completed a task within the allotted time, there is a problem. I do this when I am uncertain as to how I should approach the task. I tell myself that I must think about it to determine the best approach. I tell myself I must make time later, but I do not commit or specify what day or time later.

What have you been successful at?

I have been successful at selling, publishing, creating and marketing new services.

Have you ever felt like a failure? If so, why?

Yes, because immediately upon the failure of a project, it is difficult to separate the demise of the project from that of the person experiencing it. However, the courage and intelligence required to undertake a new project or business was not a mistake. Mistakes were made either in judgment of the opportunity or in measuring its capacity. I know there is more benefit than loss in each failure. The real power lies in a person's ability to accept failure, learn from it and realize the lessons life is teaching. Some degree of failure is necessary to help one navigate toward the pinnacle of success. People fail because they do not plan properly.

What makes you believe you will be successful in your profession and in your personal life?

I believe I will be successful in my personal life and in my business because I have failed before, picked up the pieces and maintained enthusiasm for business and life, and maintained a positive outlook toward myself, God and others.

Why would you be inclined to accept advice from people?

My respect for their specific area of expertise or experience causes me to both accept and reject advice from people. I rarely share my goals and desires with unproductive or negative people.

Do you need the approval or acceptance of a loved one in order to proceed with your goals?

No. I cannot expect a loved one to share, completely, or fully understand the course of life that was designed specifically for me. I am discovering more about this blueprint each day.

Do you feel that if you can't do something perfectly, you won't challenge it at all?

No. Success rarely requires perfection at the upstart.

Are you a perfectionist?

No. However, I will not accept mediocrity. There is substantial room between the two.

Do you have any fears?

Yes. I have most fears that others experience. I overcome them by the diagnosis I mentioned previously. I apply the prescriptions more. Consequently, I feel fewer fears each day. I am aware of them and prepared to do battle with them whenever and wherever we meet.

What does this statement mean to you: "Determination Equals Success!"

Success is in the heart. If the desire is in my heart, only death can stop it from materializing and even then, the makings to my dream can be carried on.

What advice do you have for overcoming doubt, fear and procrastination?

Study books, materials and instruction for overcoming them—if one cannot commit to do that, one is committed to failure.

Mary Kay Schreiber

Mary Kay Schreiber is president and co-founder of Orion Special Events, a corporate event and meeting planning firm located in Southern California. Under her leadership, the company has earned a reputation for outstanding creativity and results. Her client list includes Abbey Home Health Care, ESPN, Golden State Foods, NAPA Auto Parts, Pacific Care, Texaco, and Toshiba.

Prior to founding Orion, Ms. Schreiber was the Public Relations Representative for Weight Watchers of Orange, San Bernardino, Riverside and San Diego Counties in Southern California.

Mary Kay and her husband Bill have three children, ages 8, 13 and 15. They currently reside in the Los Angeles area. Her hobbies are home decorating, traveling, and singing.

What is your definition of doubt, fear, and pro-crastination?

Fear is an internal thing for me, and it is a hindrance. In terms of business, I think procrastination is a product of fear. I find that I don't procrastinate so much out of habit as much as I procrastinate out of fear, itself. Doubt also stems from fear; particularly, fear of how people will perceive you. Fear can be a negative feeling that creeps in and twists things around.

Are you always aware of the symptoms that cause you doubt, fear and procrastination?

I am becoming more aware of the symptoms. I believe that most perfectionists have those traits. I am constantly in self-evaluation. "How was that encounter with that person I just walked away from? How was that presentation? How did I present myself? How did I dress? How was I perceived?" Because of that process, I am very much aware of the symptoms. I think the more awareness I have, the more success I will have.

Are your symptoms more psychological, physio-logical, or are they a combination of both?

I would say my symptoms are more physiological. The symptoms manifest themselves through my gaining weight. Working for Weight Watchers helped me gain an awareness. I did go to therapy. I am not one of those people who is afraid to say, "I went to therapy." To me, it is just like education: college, seminars, and conventions. Therapy is a place to have another professional help you gain some insight.

When do you find yourself putting things off?

There are a couple of scenarios. One is the fear of rejection. For example, when stretching into new levels of what our company does, taking the next step up is very scary. When I started in the business all of our clients were in the Inland Empire. The jobs were very small; I was learning. I was so afraid to start marketing in Orange County; I was worried that I wasn't good enough. I was afraid to put myself out there. The truth is, we have done great in Orange County, once I pushed myself and made it happen. It wasn't my abilities that held me back, it was my personal and mental limitations that caused me to be fearful. It was easier to be a big fish in a little pond than a little fish in a big pond. Stretching beyond that was a little scary.

I have always put myself out there. If I failed, I analyzed what happened. I am very open to understanding what I didn't do well, or where I could have excelled better. You have to be willing to take a risk; that is how you push yourself to the next step.

What brings you the most success?

I am most successful with my human-to-human relationships, and am gifted with an understanding of other people.

I have been successful in overcoming obstacles. When I take on projects that seem somehow impossible, my clients, or people who are believing in me, are a driving force that steers me on the road to success. If people are depending on me, giving up is not an alternative.

How can others acquire that skill?

I listen to the people around me. I study people's body language. What are they saying to me with their bodies? What are they saying to me with their eyes, rather than with their words? If you will observe all of those things, you will really go a long way.

When I meet with clients, I can tell how they feel about what I am saying by watching their body language, their eyes, their movement, or their silence. That insight has allowed me to open doors through establishing good people-to-people relationships. I not only do that with my clients, I like to do that with the attendant at Burger King, or with the gal who is selling me art work or matting for some pictures.

I feel that every encounter you have is the whole of what your life is. If those encounters are positive, they will come back to you. They come back in a smile from someone.

In the old days, I was afraid to share, because I was afraid of the competition. Now when people call with questions, I am very happy to share information. I am not going to give what my profits and losses are, but when people who are thinking of going into the business call me, I share, because I wish I could have had someone to talk to when I was first starting out.

Is there anyone in your life who makes you feel like a success?

I had a boss who was the wife of the president of Weight Watchers. Whatever ideas I brought to the table, she thought were incredible and she was willing to invest her money. I have never had anybody else make me feel that way.

Are you good at giving control to others?

I have worked at it and, yes I am good at giving control to others. In the past, I have been afraid to give control to others, because maybe they wouldn't do the job as well as I, or maybe they would do it better. I have learned to let go and to be willing to let other people make mistakes and grow, as I have. No one can do a job 100 percent.

The more the company grows, the more I am directly involved with each project. On a creative end I still guide the projects, and as a team we come together. I start them out. I am finding that more and more, people are coming to me and saying, "Do you have a minute?" I feel it is my job to say, "Sure, do you want to talk right now?" I find that I have less and less things at my desk. Three years ago everything was *me based*, and now it is not that way. I used to feel that if I didn't have my fingers into everything, it wouldn't be done right. I am no longer afraid of delegating.

Do you allow others to assign value or self-worth to you?

Yes and no. Yes, that creeps in, and no, I choose not to let it happen. It helps to separate between what is business and what is personal. Many times I would take a rejection on a proposal as personal, and it had nothing to do with me. I can't go home and let it ruin my whole weekend, because it wasn't a personal assessment.

What makes you accept advice from people?

As we keep evolving through life, we keep changing our definition of who we are. We should never discount feelings. I have had people say things that hurt, but the truth is, they were right. As much as it hurt, it fit. I think that as you define yourself, there is advice that fits and advice that doesn't fit. It goes along with how you define your philosophies. I have even had a therapist with whom I disagreed. I didn't take what he said at face value. Now I take the advice, wear it and think, "Does that fit me?" If it does, I adopt it—it becomes part of my philosophy.

Are other people's opinions important to you?

It doesn't weigh heavily on my mind, but it feels good. I think that is what motivates people. Sometimes I struggle with that. I wonder how much is *approval*

176

based, and how much is *me based*. I think it is like the little child wanting his parent's approval. It is wonderful to have people's accolades and approval, however, if that is your only motivation, then it becomes a negative thing. You are constantly being guided by the approval or disapproval of people, and then you are in a victim's situation.

Do you need approval of a loved one in order to proceed with your goals?

No I don't. My approach is usually to work out a compromise, so it is a win-win situation.

Do you feel that if you can't do something perfectly, you won't challenge it at all?

In the past it was a constant struggle. Perfection and excellence are two different things. I work to strive toward excellence.

Can you define success?

Business success means nothing if you don't have home success. Learning balance is difficult. The element that drives you is what continues to push you. The truth is, success in business can push you away from happiness. Success is sort of like an aphrodisiac. Everything has to be in moderation. I think a lot of what makes people successful is that they are so driven. Entrepreneurs, by nature, aren't driven by finance, they are driven by accomplishment.

You should not equate your success with money. It is part of the formula, but it is not the main part of the formula.

177

What advice do you have for overcoming doubt, fear and procrastination?

You, and you alone, hold the key to stepping beyond that door. Once you step beyond that door, be prepared. There are many more doors.

Carlease Burke

Carlease Burke moved nine years ago from New York to California, with nothing—no friends, no job. She had received her bachelor of arts degree with a major in pre-law, but she had always wanted to act. So she set out to become an actress. She has succeeded in building a wonderful and still promising acting career, and she is a successful stand-up comedian.

A gifted performer, Carlease has tickled funny bones from Los Angeles to New York, with an occasional stop in Oklahoma, while sharing her offbeat, irreverent brand of comedy at The Comedy Store and other top comedy clubs throughout the United States. She has also appeared on *Roseanne, NYPD Blue, Melrose Place, Chicago Hope, Civil Wars, Knots Landing, Sisters, Life Goes On, Who's the Boss?, The Young and the Restless*, and numerous TV movies of the week.

Carlease, an accomplished singer and dancer, has been featured in the films, *Get Shorty*, and *Pie in the*

Overcoming Doubt, Fear and Procrastination

Sky. She recently appeared in the movie, *It's Pat!* with *Saturday Night Live* star Julia Sweeney.

Her stage work includes roles in the world premier of *Dreamers, Shakin' the Mess Outta Misery, For Colored Girls...,* the Los Angeles Music Center on Tour production of *Rob Bowers and the Rock Salt Company,* South Coast Repertory's *Mountains & Molehills,* and the New Heritage Theater of New York's production of *Striver's Row.*

Do you ever experience fear as an actress and a comedian?

I think I have more fear when it comes to stand-up comedy than being an actress. When I do stand-up comedy, I'm up there by myself; I want the audience to like me and accept me, but my responsibility is to make them laugh. I've been doing it all my life; I just choose to put it in a box and try to earn some money.

Generally speaking, I have no problem making people laugh. Before I perform as a comedian, I have to talk to myself. I say, "You are funny as a person." I have to remember that I am naturally funny. If I get stage fright, I have to say to myself, "You've done this before, you've been doing this for four years. You're good at it, you know what you are doing. You've performed for all types of people."

Sometimes I have to get mad at myself, and say, "What is the matter with you? You know what you are doing. Have some faith in yourself. Why are you wimping out?" Then I always say, "Lord, okay, here we go." He's always there. I don't feel like I'm walking on that stage by myself. I know I'm not up there by myself.

I was afraid of comedy in the beginning because stand-up comedy was never anything I ever thought I would be doing in my life. I never considered it as a choice for me. It was always something that entertained me. When you see other people doing things that you may have thought of, it gives you fire. It makes you feel that you can do it, and that's why role models are so important. There came a point in Hollywood when everyone was doing stand-up comedy. I read a book about it and did all the exercises, but I was still too afraid to get up on the stage, so I took a comedy class. As part of the class I had to perform at a comedy club and was provided a video-tape of my act. That's what made me get up on stage.

Sometimes you have to break the fear down into little pieces, because you may be afraid of the whole thing, but you may not be afraid of the little pieces. When we complete that one little goal that we take for granted, we don't stop and take time to pat ourselves on the back. We need to reward ourselves for taking every little step along the way.

Is there anyone in your life who makes you feel like a success?

Mark Maxwell Smith is responsible for me doing stand-up comedy. He's responsible for me hanging in there when I wanted to give up. He saw something in me. He saw the light that I have and the possibilities, motivation and energy. He has been constantly pushing me in the right direction. He writes some of my material. He helps me to feel good about myself, and he has always been there.

Do you equate success with money?

I don't think material things make you who you are, or make you any better than anyone. It may show that you are financially successful. You could drive up in a Rolls Royce. I don't know if that is your car, if you rented it, stole it, or if you live in it. It doesn't tell me anything about you as a person. I think there are all levels of success. According to society, you may look at people and determine because they appear to have a lot of money that they are successful. I don't necessarily agree with that.

Have you ever felt like a failure?

Yes, I have felt like a failure on many occasions. It is kind of hard being in the entertainment industry. For example, when I go on an audition and don't get the part, at one time I would feel like a failure. I have learned not to take it personally. After a while you realize that you are going to be told *no* more times than *yes*, and you realize it is not your fault, you just didn't get the part. I have felt like a failure at moments of rejection. If something was really important to me that I wanted and that I went after, and it didn't work out, I would feel like a failure. If there was one area of my life that I felt was the weakest, if I could use that word, that I needed the most help in, it would be in relationships with the opposite sex.

Does the opinion of others regarding your ability to become successful weigh heavily on your mind?

Let me put it like this. The more you tell me I can't and I won't, the harder I'm going to work to prove you don't know what you are talking about. The Bible says that the race does not go to the swiftest, but to the one who endures to the end. So as long as I get there, the race has been won, as far as I'm concerned.

Do you need the approval or acceptance of a loved one in order to proceed with your goals?

No, absolutely not. It would be nice. I want to think that the people I love and care about are in my

182

corner. But it doesn't always happen that way, and that could cause me to fail. If you know what you are capable of, then nobody is going to be able to stop you.

When do you especially feel good about yourself?

I feel especially good about myself in rehearsal, during and after performing, when I've made a whole bunch of people laugh, when I've done something invigorating, like exercise, when I accomplished a goal or something that I thought I never could do. I feel good about myself when I'm in church. I feel great when I talk to a friend, especially a good friend, somebody who makes me feel good. I feel good about myself when I help somebody. I feel good when I motivate and inspire people.

When do you feel bad about yourself?

Well, this hardly ever happens, but the first thing that comes to mind is that I feel bad about myself when I'm lonely. I'm hardly ever lonely, but there are times. Sometimes everything comes to a halt; I may not have a relationship, and I may not be working or auditioning. Sometimes things get quiet, but that's how I've learned to enjoy leisure time and have balance in my life. Balance is important.

What has brought you the most success?

When I first came out here nine years ago, I was working temporary jobs for $5-6 an hour. Now I support myself solely as an entertainer. I've succeeded in becoming a stand-up comedian who is starting to get paid a little bit more. I have received some awards in acting. I have done some creative writing. I received a screenplay award for a film that I co-wrote, called, *The Follower Out of New York.* I've succeeded in becoming a competent toastmaster in one year. I wanted to embark on a public speaking career. I've succeeded in being confident in who I am and liking who I am. There is always room for growth.

I have succeeded in educating myself. I went to college to please my parents, but I am glad that I have a bachelor of arts degree. I have wanted to act my whole life. That's a dream, a goal, that I have had from childhood, and now I'm doing it; I'm living my dream.

I have succeeded in becoming a Christian. I feel that I have been a Christian my whole life, and I am not ashamed of it. I want to be a good witness to people.

Derek Scott

Derek Scott was raised in southern California. At age 19, he served as a missionary in Brazil for two years, teaching others about the Gospel of Jesus Christ. He then went to Brigham Young University in Utah.

After college, Derek and his wife Leslie decided to move to southern Utah where they felt the atmosphere was conducive to raising their four daughters.

Derek went to work for John Clemons, owner of LearnKey, a software training video business. Derek soon worked his way up to director of operations. He works hard for LearnKey, but his family is his first priority and he loves spending time with them, especially in the outdoors. Their favorite recreation is water skiing in Southern Utah.

Derek is very modest about his success. He says, *I think I am the epitome of the average, red-blooded American boy now grown up. From my youth on up I have tasted successes and failures, moments of praise and humiliation, five-star dining to dumpster dining, international business travel to ranch-hand laborer, romantic rendezvous to dirty diapers.*

Through it all, I, like most of the other millions, with just slightly different size shoes or circumstances, just keep plugging away. Our lives and stories are so usual and common that they are seldom told—nothing too eventful, but usually more meaningful and important than the stories that make the 5 o'clock news. We are the ones who are content to make things work without all the hoopla. A hug from a child, kiss from the wife, and recognition from the boss are rewards that make getting up in the morning and overcoming doubt, fear and procrastination all worthwhile.

How did you prepare yourself to step in and become the director of operations for LearnKey?

Well, that's easy. I was at BYU getting my prerequisites for dentistry. I decided that poking my fingers in people's mouths all day was not for me, so I went into sociology. I loved it! I got A's for the first time in my college career—I got straight A's all the way in my new major. I have always liked being involved with people, and have worked hard to complete any task or assignment I have been given.

What are the pros and cons of your profession?

I see that the pros and cons mix real closely for me. It goes back to the people. A pro is that it's fun to see people enjoy what they're doing and to accomplish a task that's never been done before. For example, just this last week we gave our production crew the challenge to edit a show in one week. It was a show that we've done before, but not in one week. We said, "Let's change this and make it work." It was stressful for them, but they saw that they could do it, and I think they are now feeling some real sense of accomplishment because they did that. It's exciting to see that happen.

Derek, you flew here with John in his private plane. Did you experience feelings of fear?

I trust John because he thinks things through. We got up in the air, and all of a sudden he said, "I need to look at the map, take the wheel." That's his style; he's the same in business. He talked me through the basics I needed to know and then he said, just like in his business, "run with it." I kept looking out for planes. I guess I was pretty nervous.

John Clemons comments during the interview: *It's a pretty simple process. It's just that most people make it out to be more complicated than it is. Flying the plane, once you get it up there, is really quite simple. The key to keeping Derek from getting overly nervous was to tell him what was happening, and I kept telling him how well he was flying the machine. We basically have a line from St. George to Chino and we just fly that line, and keep it at a certain pace.*

Derek, what is your definition of doubt, fear, and procrastination?

To me, doubt is forgetting that I have inherited self-worth and that all things are possible if I have the desire and search for help from appropriate sources. Fear is losing sight or not knowing what my goals or beliefs are. Once these are established, a lack of preparation periodically causes me fear. Procrastination is the result of doubt and fear, if not controlled. It is putting off for no worthy reason what needs to be done.

Are you always aware of the symptoms?

Yes, but that does not mean that I always avoid the symptoms. I have weakness and when I stop striving to achieve or when I say or do something I know to be less than what I expect of myself, I experience doubt, fear, and procrastination. I am not perfect and try not to beat up on myself too much when I miss my mark (I am a Christian and believe in forgiveness). As long as I am learning from my mistakes and am not always repeating the same ones, I feel accomplishment.

What has brought you success?

I used to take pride in the athletic awards I earned in high school, but they lost their shine and impressiveness the further I got from my graduation date and high school peers. Closing seemingly big business deals with an import company and worldly travels appeared to be my next source of pride right out of college.

The older I get, I'm beginning to understand the dangers and pitfalls of measuring success by the bumper sticker, *He who dies with the most toys [or largest bank account] wins.* When I scour my memory, I find myself savoring the most simple pleasures and private successes.

First comes to mind my relationship with Leslie, my wife, and our four daughters. Caring for, teaching and directing our young ones provide more sense of accomplishment than anything else that we have encountered. No business deal has been as enjoyable or rewarding as seeing our children's first steps, excitement in their eyes upon writing their names, or first solo bike rides.

A successful marriage is very rewarding and quite the rarity today in America. And some successes, like a marriage, are never complete. They require constant work and care, and we are more successful sometimes than others. Failure in this area is not an option. Just as we would not abandon an unruly child, we as parents will not abandon them by abandoning each other. The relationships developed with my parents and hers, as well as with brothers and sisters, take work but have great rewards.

I spent two years as a missionary in Brazil helping and teaching others. This is a very quiet and deep well of accomplishment. Also, the jobs I have had that I mastered and felt appreciated have brought me satisfaction. I've done construction and landscaping, and have felt a great sense of accomplishment in seeing a job well done. Now in the video training business I feel the same sense of achievement in seeing a well-produced show, catalog, etc.

Relationships, trust and bonds of friendship developed only as side effects of doing business, I remember more and enjoy more than the money or deals made in business. Judging from others' comments and seeing the relationships that great men and women develop, I think character, values, and sound beliefs are better measures of success than deals and dollars.

Paul Harvey's *The Rest of the Story* series is replete with individuals who were not deemed successful until after their death. Even the greatest to walk this earth, Jesus Christ, would not be considered "successful" by today's standards.

Is there anyone in your life who makes you feel like a success?

Loved ones and friends help me feel successful. Strangers or acquaintances may be impressed by me or some accomplishments, but I see this more as an ego thing than real success. Folks who don't know me well enough to know what "makes me tick," may be impressed with some external, visible, or materialistic sort of "success" when the real valuable things may not be seen or recognized. I see this all the time with John Clemons. People are impressed with things a successful business allows one to acquire, not knowing at all why LearnKey has been successful.

Have you ever felt like a failure?

Yes, when it appeared I did not have the ability to perform a test. I believe people fail because of a lack of direction, training or motivation. I do remember re-evaluating two areas I felt like a failure in, trigonometry and organic chemistry in college. Typically, I have been able to re-commit myself through study, work, practice or just another try. When I did not have the motivation, desire or drive to succeed, I re-evaluated my goals and decided the additional work necessary to succeed would not make me happy. I was struggling with the means for a goal that I did not want. Once I re-set my goals, I had tremendous success in the social sciences and realized what would make me happy.

What makes you believe you will be successful in your professional and personal life?

I must put my personal life first. Don't get me wrong. I put in great time and effort for LearnKey, but I have to keep things in perspective, and that means family comes before profession.

In my personal life, I have a "don't look back attitude." We dated a lot of people before meeting and marrying, so Leslie and I had the blinders off when seeing our relationship. We talked extensively about what individual likes, dislikes and goals we had, and knew we were in agreement with important issues before making what we believe is an endless commitment.

In my profession, as long as I am willing to work hard, I will achieve minimal success and a decent income to support my family. With employer or without, if I can be a part of providing a good or service that is better than expected, I will achieve superior success.

Please share what this statement mean to you: "Determination equals success!"

I think it is a true concept; the *never quit* mentality is very good. The question is, what degree of success do I wish to attain and at the expense of what do I become successful? I believe *wisdom* must come into play at some point to give direction and to temper one's drive for success.

Gail Blake-Smith

Gail Blake Smith was born and raised in Los Angeles, California. She and her husband Tommy, currently reside in Southern California. She spent 26 years in a career position with Pacific Bell as a Human Resources Manager.

One of her greatest interests is international traveling. She and her husband have ventured to many countries, such as England, France, Germany, Monaco, the Netherlands, Belgium, Egypt, Italy, and Israel.

If you were lecturing to a group of people, how would you explain worry?

We usually have very little control over the situation or circumstance. Worry is something that is inherent in the human population, and it tends to escalate or de-escalate, depending on the attitude and the biological makeup of the individuals. It is a condition or a phenomenon, based upon a situation or a series of situations which can be compounded, depending upon how an individual feels and reacts toward that situation. It has to do with faith systems, belief systems, or lack of them.

Do you tend to put things off?

No, I probably drive everyone I know crazy. I usually get everything done early, including my Christmas shopping. I think a lot of it comes from 30 years of working for a large corporation and being taught punctuality and how to manage time, and the value of being proactive, as far as managing my time. Just as we budget money, we need to learn how to budget time; if we don't, we are going to feel stressed and worried, and from my perspective it seems to be more of a gender issue. Men tend to procrastinate more than women. Even when I'm on vacation, I make a list to make sure that I accomplish my goals. It has to do with being goal-oriented. Men usually try to remember everything—then they forget. Most men wait until Christmas Eve to go Christmas shopping. I have fears and doubts from time to time, and I deal with them, but I rarely ever procrastinate. I've got to do it, so I might as well get it over with.

You've made some wise investments. How can someone overcome the fear of investing?

Well, no one is going to get rich just working for a company, let's face it. If there's an opportunity to invest in an investment plan at work, you should get into it right away. I've been in it for 20 years. I probably lost about 1/2 million dollars in stock. So that would be my number one advice, to look at those things within your company, or your business, where you can invest. If you save a dollar a week when you're in your 20s, by the time you retire, you are going to be financially secure. Savings: You should take advantage of any kind of profit sharing or savings plan offered through your job; if you don't want to go through your job, save on your own. Pennies add up. Just go into it very, very conservatively at first, as I did. Find what you like, take some action, but make prudent investment decisions, and from there evaluate on an ongoing basis. Ask yourself, "Do I stay with what I'm doing? Do I add to it? Do I shift?" Don't let fear be an issue, because the only thing to fear, of course, is fear itself. Take some action, even if you fail. Failure can be healthy.

Were you afraid at first?

I thought I'd miss the money and that I couldn't afford it—those were my fears. I bought an apartment building and thought it would pay better returns than investing at work, but it didn't. My sister-in-law told me to try investing 2% in the investment plan at work, and I did. I didn't miss it, so I got more aggressive; I went to 4%, then to 6%, and then to 16%.

Gail, you get a phone call from your friend, Veda. She's distraught, and feeling like a failure. How can you help her?

First, I think I would try to make her feel good about herself. I would try to build her self-esteem and give her hope; if she is beaten down, she is not going to be of value to anyone. I would work on Veda's self-esteem and attitude. Once she feels better about herself and is ready to do whatever is necessary to climb the steps to success, then she can start looking squarely at the problem. She can ask herself, "What can I segregate, what do I want to save, what's more important, what's high priority, and what's low on my list?" Then she can start tackling each task in that order.

Why can't people isolate themselves and do that for themselves?

They are too close to the situation. They just can't be objective at that point. They are too involved and too subjective. They need to step away from the situation and look at the things that are preventing them from meeting their goals. They need to identify the problems and take one problem a day, or perhaps just one problem a week. It helps to break the obstacle down into segments, rather than trying to tackle it in its totality, which can be overwhelming, causing more feelings of inadequacy and failure.

For example, take a household where you are having problems with your spouse, your kids, your bills, and maybe even your contractors. You just have to deal with each problem individually, head on. You have to have a plan of attack, a tactical or strategic plan for each case. First, how are you going to improve your relationship with your spouse? Then, how can you help your kids improve? How can you better budget your money to pay your bills in a more timely fashion? And, how are you going to deal with the vendors? You could look at the whole set of circumstances and cry, become dependent upon liquor, run away, regress, get depressed, break down, or give up. Instead, you need to solve one issue at a time and then go to the next one; you may even lose sometimes. Maybe all problems aren't solvable. We need to recognize that, accept it, and go on to something at which we can succeed.

Have you ever felt like a failure?

Yes. It was more of a personal nature. My feeling of failure or inadequacy had to do with my relationships with men. I failed constantly, for more than twenty years, however, I was totally in control of the failure.

Overcoming Doubt, Fear and Procrastination

When did you recognize the problem?

Probably in my late thirties. I had to look at what was causing the problem. It was the kind of people I associated with. The kind I was attracted to were not ready to settle down and have a relationship—just fun. I was out there for fun, but in the back of my mind I had a hidden agenda, and they didn't buy into it. I felt like a big failure for a number of years in my relationships with men.

I finally said, "Lord, if you want me to get married, it's up to you. I just want to have peace and follow your guidance." And then I would pray, "Oh, God, I don't want to get involved in another relationship." But, you know, you just mature in the Lord and have faith anyway, because I didn't get married until I was 46. The chances of that happening for the first time after 40 is under 1%. When I became engaged, I was confused about what love was, and I'm still defining it everyday. I think maturity and being single for 46 years, twenty-some-odd years as an adult, and seeing different sides of people, helped me to see things that are important. Everything that glitters isn't gold, and I used to think it was. As I have matured, so have my values.

Do you have any fear of confrontation?

I took a Myers, Strongberg, and Carlson personality test twice, and the one area of weakness in my personality that was common on both examinations, was that of conflict.

Would you want to delegate the handling of confrontations to someone else?

Yes, I am not real natural at it. I have to deal with an issue concerning a tenant tomorrow, and I have to tell her that her dog has to go. I don't want to hurt her, and I don't want her to move, but other tenants are complaining. She has been there eight years and has been an ideal tenant. She bought the dog for her grandson, and it's going to break his heart; and I worry about the dog. How am I going to handle it? I'll pray on it, because the Lord will lead me. But it has to be done. I'm procrastinating on calling her. When I go home, I have to do it, even though I don't want to do it.

You have been successful; can you tell us about your accomplishments?

I have been successful at balancing my life. I have had a successful career. I was a human resource manager for Pacific Bell. I started as a file clerk. I just wanted to work long enough to get a car. I worked my way up through management without a college degree, and when I left I was in middle management. I was able to retire at 46 with a pension for life, and all the benefits that go with retirement.

I think it is important to help other people. To me, there is no greater compensation than the feeling that comes from providing a service, a word of encouragement, a card, or helping someone through a hardship. I believe those arc the things that we are going to take with us from this life that will be counted. In addition, I feel that I have been successful at providing good family values as the matriarch of my family, and being the cheerleader for the family.

Don L. Price

Don L. Price is a speaker, author, marketing and sales strategist. He is the author of *Secrets of Personal Marketing Power: Strategies for Achieving Greater Personal & Business Success.* This dynamic book serves as a primary resource for individuals and businesses seeking to maximize their profit potential. Don demonstrates commitment, creativity, and enthusiasm in his programs. He has shared his skills and insights about personal marketing power with more than 40,000 sales and marketing professionals across the nation. His articles on marketing have been published nationally.

Don's message of self-promotion, personal empowerment, business-building strategies, and success are profitable and beneficial for everyone from beginners to the most seasoned professionals. He developed his extensive personal marketing know-how during his thirty-plus years of high-level corporate experience in marketing, sales training, and management.

A resident of Redondo Beach, California, Don is a member of the National Speakers Association and is listed in *Who's Who in Professional Speaking.*

Have you ever experienced doubt, fear, and procrastination?

I am sure that I have. I don't experience them to the degree where I get overly concerned. I'm less of a procrastinator now because I have more of an interest. I have more of a mission, and I am more focused on where I want to go. I think people procrastinate because they don't know where they are going. I think they are kind of in disarray. Vector-splatter is what I call it. The last ten years have probably been my best years in life, in terms of having a very specific direction, goals, and a mission of things I want to accomplish. When we get a little older we begin to think differently.

Are you always aware of the symptoms?

Yes, I am very aware of the symptoms. When I feel myself hesitating, I look at it not necessarily as fear or procrastination, but as doubt. Perhaps I don't have enough information, or maybe I need to be a little more thorough or get more information to take care of a project.

Fear—sometimes I should have a little fear to stop me. At times I think that I am fearless, especially when it comes to going out and speaking before a group. That's one thing I don't have a fear of, and I don't know if that's an over-compensation of another characteristic trait or what, but I don't have a fear in that area.

Do you feel that you have been successful?

During my early thirties I had the desire to start writing. I've always written poetry. I have also written journals, educational programs, curriculums and tape programs for companies. I have co-authored a book with a friend, and it has become very successful. That motivated me to write my own book, *Secrets of Personal Marketing.* I think that I have been successful in accomplishing that goal and objective. Quite frankly, I believe the book is going to be very successful. When I was working for Pepsi Cola Bottling Company, I was successful at the corporate level. I think I am a successful speaker. I consider myself a successful illustrator and an accomplished painter. I don't believe that anyone ever arrives at utopia. I believe that I am always learning and moving forward.

Is there anyone in your life who makes you feel like a success?

I do have a lot of people who say they admire what I have accomplished. I came from a family of seven children. I was the person who stood out the most in terms of reaching goals, success and accomplishments, which doesn't mean that the others haven't succeeded in their own right. Basically, I make myself feel successful. I don't know if anyone can really make you feel successful.

Have you ever felt like a failure?

I think there are many times when I have attempted something and did not accomplish my goal. I don't carry that baggage around. I am more of a winner in life and feel good about the way I do things.

I take a look at it from a realistic point of view, and ask myself, "Where can I take responsibility for the failure? Was it the planning stage that didn't work out for me? Was it in my commitment? Did I really want it?"

After I go through a lot of assessment with my-self, I let it go, and then I move on with my life. There is not enough time in this world to get caught up in the baggage we force upon ourselves.

What do you think causes people to fail?

I believe people fail because of a lack of commit-ment, self-esteem, self-confidence, and not having a goal in mind. I believe success is something you have to look at as a continuum and journey. Most people don't stick around long enough to see success.

Some people have had their parents tell them to be a doctor, an attorney or something thcy didn't want to be, but they did it for their parents. They've hated it from the beginning and have been miserable. You have to have a vision and passion and go after what it is you want to do.

What makes you believe you will be successful in your professional and personal life?

In my profession, I am a success now. I will con-tinue to be a success as the journey rolls on. I have a great passion for my work, and I like what I do. It is not even a matter of dollars and cents; it is a matter of my own personal pride and what I can give others.

In my personal life, right now, spiritually, emo-tionally and physically, I feel great. I feel real comfort-able. I am in a real good place in life. I can honestly say there are not any real problems. I am not married and I don't have a particular lady that I'm dating. I am just having a great time living life to the maximum, and un-derstanding what life is really about.

Are you good at giving control to others?

Yes and no. When it comes to the detailed work, I would rather have other people do it. When it comes to the major decisions, I don't like to be out of control. I like to be in that loop, constantly.

How about taking control?

I love to take control. I am a controller. I will do that constantly. In a conversation, I have a tendency to take control. Even when I feel a little bit apprehensive, if I have the ability to handle a project, I'll still take control. It's just my nature.

In order to become more successful, what would you delegate to others?

In my situation right now, there is a lot that I could delegate. I think a lot has to do with finding the right people, who I have complete confidence and trust in, and who think pretty much the way I do in terms of priorities. I am becoming more inclined to trust people. If I could trust people more to follow through, and to do so with care and responsibility, I would probably be more successful at delegating.

Are the opinions of others important to you?

When I was younger, my peer group's opinions were more important to me than the opinions of my superior group or subordinates. Today, I don't need the approval or acceptance of others.

Is the approval or acceptance of a loved one important in order to proceed with your goals?

I don't need it, but I do like it. I like to have the approval of those around me who love me and believe in me, to say, "Hey, we really support you and we believe in you." No, I don't need it, but I'll tell you, it sure is nice having that extra support, because it can take you through some bumpy roads in your career.

When do you especially feel good about yourself?

I feel good about myself when I can walk away from a presentation and know that at least fifty to sixty percent of the audience got value. I know one thing in life: I cannot satisfy all of the people all of the time, but I can satisfy some of the people, some of the time. I understand and accept that, even though I will try to satisfy all of the people all of the time. When I accomplish my goals, when I know that I've just about hit the peak, that's when I feel good about myself.

When do you feel bad about yourself?

I feel bad when I've cheated myself or when I haven't given my very best.

Do you have any fears?

I have more concerns than I have fear. Right now my fears are world conditions. I see what is going on, and I fear for others more than I fear for myself. I fear for children. Someone said the other night on television that this country does not support the children of the world, nor do we support the children of the United States. He brought up a very good example. He said that we support prisoners more than we support our children. Most prisoners have better standards of living and education inside the prison walls, than our students have today in secondary education. I fear that we are a society heading for some terrible times. We don't have respect for one another anymore. I see that as a real problem.

What advice do you have for overcoming doubt, fear and procrastination?

Learn who you are, and what capabilities you have. Be proud of who you are and build on that pride.

Alice Wright

Alice Yavonnia Wright currently owns and operates various businesses. In 1979 she started working in the areas of Insurance, Investments, Financial Planning, and Business Management. In 1981 she opened a residential care facility for developmentally disabled children and has continued servicing their needs, though they are now adults. In 1992 she started providing residential rentals in California and purchased a trucking company, servicing areas throughout the United States.

Ms. Wright earned a bachelor of science degree in business administration from California State University at Long Beach and completed the certified financial planner program at the University of Southern California at Los Angeles/College for Financial Planning in Denver.

Ms. Wright is registered with the National Association of Securities Dealers (NASD). She is also licensed in Variable Contracts, Life and Disability, and Fire and Casualty. Also, she is a registered investment advisor.

She works with small businesses and individuals to help them become more successful through proper handling of money and business matters.

Organization and memberships present and past include the International Association for Financial Planning (IAFP), National Association of University Women (NAUW), and Society of California Care Home Operators (SOCCO). In addition to servicing the needs of the developmentally disabled, she is active in community affairs.

Have you always been successful?

I have been successful at a lot of things. While I was growing up, my mother involved us in everything from Woodcraft Rangers to Girl Scouts, along with all kinds of sports, such as softball and baseball. We did a multitude of things. When I was younger I was heavily involved in track and field. I broke established records in the fifty-yard relay. I also received scholastic awards and awards in music while attending school.

Have you ever been afraid of a challenge?

No. A challenge keeps me from getting bored. I do things to keep from being bored. My first business was residential care. I felt as if I were playing the game of business, until problems or challenges came up. Then things became serious. I opened the first business, the residential care, in 1981, and the second, Kamonie Financial, in 1986.

When I opened Kamonie Financial, I opened it without any clients. Even though I had clients from working with other companies, I didn't count on them coming with me. My mother was the one who said, "We're going to have a small office warming," and sure enough, I picked up a couple of clients.

If you have the education and the initiative to do whatever has to be done, then you can make it. It's not about sitting, hoping and praying that it's going to happen. You've got to have some oomph, also.

How did you get started in the trucking business?

I ended up with a large sum of money that I had to get rid of fast. I bought an apartment building, but I still needed to get rid of more money. My brother had been in trucking for about seven years at that time, and I wanted to give him a gift. I said, "Let me buy you a truck." He said, "Let's set up a trucking company." It was okay with me, because it was a write-off for me. I decided that even if I bought the truck and it sat there for a whole year, it would be no big deal. I could simply write it off. That's how the whole thing started. I started with one truck, and I had no idea that I would be getting more trucks. I have four now, and I'll be adding another four.

My brother got a contract from a trucking company he previously worked for, and that was the beginning of our trucking business. Then the company turned around and gave him another contract for another route. Last month they called and asked me to come in for a meeting. They are giving our company the entire state of Texas. So now we have Oklahoma and Texas. There are only a couple of stores in Oklahoma, but eventually Oklahoma will expand. They have asked our company to run a local truck out of Chicago, but we're still thinking about that.

Being a female in a male-dominated business, have you had any problems with people taking you seriously?

No, because as far as they know, I'm just an administrative assistant. When they hear a female voice over the phone, it is usually the person who is booking the loads, and they don't ask who owns the company. When I start faxing the paperwork to them, then they can see who owns it, but they usually don't say anything. As far as they know, it is just Alice and she is booking the loads.

Do you have any advice for those who want to start a new venture?

You must be open for new opportunities. I have found in dealing with some people that opportunity can knock at the door and they won't even open it; they never even knew it came. Say you have been trying to get a certain contract, maybe you don't get the whole contract, but if you can at least get your foot in the door, take it, even though it may be for a little less money then you wanted, a few less hours, or not exactly the route you wanted. You wanted to go south and they are sending you north. Once you are in the door, you can maneuver things all kinds of ways.

I have found that everything is negotiable. When a person tells me something can't be done, I want to know why.

You have your feet firmly planted in this business, and you can expand your business with a certain level of comfort, because you have built a foundation.

Right. In Kamonie Financial, 98 percent of my clients are small business owners. I am dealing with different types of businesses, but the foundation is still the same. You get basics down; whether it is residential care, rentals, trucking, or a consulting firm, things are still going to run the same. The bottom line is that you want to make a profit. Some things are basic and you have to do whatever it takes in order to make it work.

You can start out and everything can be booming, but you need to think ahead. This is your good season now, but when is your bad season? You need to find out when the slow season is and be in a position to anticipate and plan ahead before you get into the middle of it.

With the residential care you don't have ups and downs. It is consistent because you are dealing with the state and social services, which are totally different from the business world. With the consulting firm, generally you have times that are up and down. Summer time is vacation time, a lot of people are going in and out of town, so it is going to take you a little longer to close some deals. In the trucking industry, with the products that we carry, the winter time is a slower time.

You have four healthy, solid businesses. How do you balance your personal and professional life?

It can become overwhelming, if you let it. The first thing is organization. As you can see, I am sitting here in front of you with my appointment book. I have one appointment book. I get the same one every year, because it starts at 7:00 a.m. and goes to 8:45 p.m.

I have a seven-month old son, and he changes things, totally. I think that a person will go through episodes of being in balance and times of being out of balance. Right now, I think that I am out of balance, because I have no time for myself. I'm running and doing what I have to do with the businesses and then spending time with my baby. Mondays and Fridays are my busiest and my longest days. When you read and follow books on how to be organized, you think they are going to keep you in balance all of the time, but they don't. I think it is important for people to understand that you are going to be out of balance sometimes, and then you are going to come back into balance.

In your opinion, what causes people to fail?

I think people fail when they are not open to new ideas. While I am trying to talk to them and give them information that may be helpful, they are so busy with their brain clicking and thinking negatively, that they don't even hear what I am saying. They end up blocking me out, and they just don't get it. That is definitely one reason for failure. Just sit there, close your mouth, and listen to what the successful people are saying. Get all of it. Wait until they stop talking; then you have plenty of time to sit there and let your brain click. Another cause for failure is lack of information. You must have information; information goes along with education.

When do you especially feel good about yourself?

I especially feel good about myself now that I have a baby. Just being able to spend time with him makes me happy. I feel good about myself when I can envision something, and then I can sit down and put it on paper. Then I can look up, and there it is; it is something that I can feel, touch, and smell.

When do you feel bad about yourself?

I feel bad sometimes when I am overwhelmed, and it really makes me tired. I don't rest well, even though I may sleep, and I don't eat properly. It is draining on me physically and mentally, and it makes me feel bad. I have to rearrange some things, not attend social events, and cancel some meetings. It is something that I have learned. When I was 20, I could party all night and still get up and run things. Now making it to 10:30 p.m. is a chore.

Overcoming Doubt, Fear and Procrastination

What advice do you have for overcoming doubt, fear and procrastination?

If thoughts of doubt run across your mind, let them run across your mind and move on. Everyone has fears about something. Look hard into those fears to see why you are fearful. My advice to a person who really procrastinates, is to just get up and do it. Push yourself to do it, if you want to be successful.

Pastor Dave Stoecklein

Pastor Dave Stoecklein was born and raised in Colby, Kansas, a small town in the northwest corner of the state. The Stoecklein family consisted of Dad and Mom, six boys and two girls.

At the age of 17, Dave became a Born Again Christian and realized God's "call" to the ministry as a vocation. After attending a couple of undergraduate schools and working in a couple of smaller churches as an intern, Dave and his wife Carol moved to Chino, California. In the fall of 1983, they were employed as youth and education directors at a local church.

After completing a master of arts degree in theology in 1986, Dave and Carol felt impressed to pioneer (plant) a brand new church in the area of Chino Hills. So, with a core group of just 13 adults, Inland Hills Church was birthed on February 3, 1991. The first public service saw 266 people in attendance. The new church was strategically developed with a target group in mind, "Chino Hills Charlie," the prolific non-churched upper/middle class baby boomer! Contemporary music, positive and practical message topics from the Bible, an exciting children's and students' program, and an atmosphere of acceptance and friendliness make up the spiritual architecture of Inland Hills.

Now, in its sixth year, Inland Hills Church has grown to 1,000 people in average attendance each Sunday. It has been recognized in two leading church growth books as well as featured in the LA. Times Magazine. Dave and Carol attribute the church's *success* to simply God's grace, being in the right place at the right time, and willing to risk everything for Kingdom Building sake.

Dave and Carol have been blessed with three children, Andrew, 8, Paige, 6, and Austin, 4. Dave's hobbies are basketball, reading, bike riding, and playing with the kids.

How did you become a Christian?

I was probably 16 or 17, and I was in high school. I had a religious upbringing, but definitely wasn't Christian. I knew the difference between right and wrong. I leaned toward perfection.

I was introduced to the fact of heaven, life after death, and eternal life by a friend. The Bible says the way to get to heaven is to accept and follow Jesus Christ. I wanted to make sure that I had accepted the Savior and what he had done, rather than just being a religious person. When no one else was around, I prayed, "God, I want to make sure I'm going to heaven. Please give me my heart and make a difference. I just want to do what you want me to do."

So I had come to grips with that, because even as a young kid and a teenager, I had different gods that would call the shots in my life: What people thought, athletics, and friends, and they were the persons who decided what I would do with my life. That's how I found my fulfillment, just through what other people thought. If I could do okay on the football field, or run track or whatever, I got the accolades there, that's fine. But in a sense, it was really God who called the shots in my life. God made me and knows me and has a plan for my life. I finally accepted that and learned how he even had a better plan for me than my own plans. I gained some friends and I gained some respect from the acquaintances.

What is your definition of worry?

Worry is negative meditation. If you worry, you dwell on something negative. If you dwell on something positive it will bring success to your life, but if you dwell on something negative, I believe that is worry.

I think I have been a victim of worry. It haunts me still, and it is a process of getting through—it comes back and then I have to use what I have used in the past to get some wind under my belt to conquer it, and slowly, in time, worry is no longer a problem for me.

Can you define doubt, fear, and procrastination?

To have doubt is to be unsure and unprepared. Fear is feeling that the worst is going to come; not knowing the predicaments of the future, and feeling that whatever will be worse, will happen. Procrastination is putting off until tomorrow what should have been done today. It is the ignorance of the moment.

As a Christian, are you better equipped to handle these issues?

Yes, at times. I think that we all have the same tools. I don't think everyone knows how to use the tools. The tools seem available and because there is so much doubt, we are not going to rely on them. It is like having all this water to put out a fire, but I just don't; I don't want to deal with it now, so I don't go for it. Just through trial and error, I have learned that I can go to those tools, and you know when a red light comes on, to put it out now, or else it's going to get worse later on.

Are you good at giving control to others?

I would delegate everything that someone else can do that I shouldn't be doing. I would delegate everything, and then I would be able to put more time into those things that I can do and no one else can do. In my area, I cannot delegate a vision, and I cannot delegate my responsibilities, so I'll give more time to those two areas, and my assistants can do everything else.

I have become good at giving control to others. I've had a setback, so that experience has made it more difficult for me to trust others in terms of giving them control. I would rather do things myself, especially starting a business. In order to grow I have to release authority and responsibility, and that means giving up control. One of the priorities with our staff is, we really believe in making a mistake—one mistake a week but not the same mistake. If you keep making the same mistake, then you have a problem; something is wrong. We think that if you are going to be successful, you need to make at least one mistake, so we can give a lot of flexibility there. We'll hit more home runs if we at least make a few mistakes. Giving control takes time, but it works for us.

If control is given to me and I am comfortable with it, I'll absolutely take control and run with it. I am an achiever, so I have no problem with taking control.

How does a person avoid failure?

The biggest cause of failure is not trying. Many people won't even try. They set some standards too high. I go back to those affirmations in my life and back to defining moments in my life when I have had success or someone has been there to say, "This is where you started from." With Christ it's all different. He says, "I would not have brought you this far to leave you right here." So when I feel like a failure I go back to Him, and that is how I get through. I really think I wouldn't be able to do it myself, so I look to the spiritual power.

Do you believe you will be successful?

I believe I will be successful in my personal life because I have accepted and admitted who I am in my relationship with God. I think by putting Him first, there is no way that I cannot be successful. In my vocation it is almost exactly the same, admitting that He is in charge. I am involved in something that is much greater than I. Accepting who I am in Christ is what makes me successful.

Who makes you feel like a success?

I think that I've probably been successful at being able to grasp a vision and communicate it with clarity. However, my wife, my immediate staff and the people who are the closest to me make me feel like a success. We have to have those people. They affirm who I am as a person and vision carrier.

Do you allow others to assign value or self-worth to you?

I can't, because my value and self-worth come from a higher source. I have to walk with what He says I am. If someone doesn't like me, that's the person's problem, not mine.

Overcoming Doubt, Fear and Procrastination

When do you feel good about yourself?

I especially feel good about myself when I am less and less dependent on what other people think. That is a huge accomplishment for me to come that far. I am much more dependent on my Maker and Creator, and I feel that I am playing my life to the audience of one. He is the one who gives me, "You are doing good, son." I feel good about that. But still, it comes back to the people who are the closest to me. I've chosen two or three people at the most to be close, and they'll usually affirm that, because you cannot see God. I still need to come back to something. He allows you to come back to someone physical in your life—someone who is tangible, that just at the right time will say, "Good job." God made us like that, and I think we need some people.

What advice do you have for overcoming doubt, fear and procrastination?

People need to come to the full realization of who they are; they were never meant to conquer the whole world by themselves. When they realize who they are, and understand their strengths and weaknesses, that's a good starting point for desire and determination. Then they need to make some decisions and stick with them. They will overcome fears, doubts, and putting things off. But when the weight is so heavy regarding failing, and what other people are going to think, then they may take several steps backwards. People need to be honest with themselves. I don't see how people can be honest with who they are when they don't deal with God. That, I think, they have to deal with. That's where I come from.

Jerrold Curry

Jerrold Curry was raised in Oakland, California. He attended Merritt Junior College and received his associate in arts degree before moving to Southern California. There he obtained a bachelor of science degree in kinesiology from Cal Poly Pomona University. He later earned his master of arts and teaching credential from Claremont Graduate School. Shortly thereafter, he started teaching for Pomona Unified School District where he continues to teach.

Added to his list of accomplishments, Mr. Curry was high school state/national champion and college all-American in track and field competition. For the past six years he has been owner of a Baskin-Robbins ice cream franchise. He is currently engaged in negotiations for ownership of another major franchise. Success seems to run in the Curry family. Jerrold is the brother of Mark Curry, star of the popular television sitcom *Hanging With Mr. Cooper.*

I have read your autobiography; you have very strong business skills.

Well, I don't see it as being strong, or extraordinary, or different. I usually go into a situation overly prepared. In other words, I give the person no reason to say no.

For example, when I was contemplating acquiring a Baskin-Robbins franchise, I felt comfortable because I was extremely prepared.

To what do you attribute your success?

I just go back to being very young and having a lack of money. However, after you make enough money, then the rest becomes a game. After you have achieved financial success, and have acquired whatever toys you need to have, then it becomes more of a power thing.

What does success mean to you?

To me, success is when your opinion is all of a sudden seen as something everyone should listen to. Success is the ability to call the shots. I was talking to the guy who services my car at the dealership and he was telling me, "Oh, you're this and you're that." I said, "No, you're successful in what you do because you're very knowledgeable, and whatever my problem is you know how to repair it, so you're just as successful. Now, what you do with that knowledge after you have it, is up to you."

Do you equate money with success?

No, not at all. But money and success kind of go hand in hand. If you're very successful at what you do, whatever it may be, there are going to be some financial rewards. It's up to you how much it is going to be. Some people aren't concerned with it.

With the success of Baskin-Robbins, has that given you the confidence to go after McDonald's?

I applied for a McDonald's franchise during the same time I applied for a Baskin-Robbins. I found a quote that the president of McDonald's said: "All you need is the ability to balance a checkbook and good people skills and we will teach you the rest." I took him at his word and when McDonald's said no, I gave them examples of other people who were football players that they let into the program. They didn't even have a college degree. I wondered if it was because they have money or notoriety. I've met their financial obligations.

The president finally sent me a letter saying they want me to have more management skills, and he suggested that I buy a liquor store and then come back. That was a way out that I didn't have any control over at the time. I still have that letter, even though that was six years ago. I'm going to hold them to their word, and I'm also going to be prepared. They only had one reason to turn me down, and they used it!

Once you acquire another franchise, what's after that?

I think the average individual can master a franchise in a couple of years. I know several franchisees who own multiple stores. Most franchisers encourage multiple ownership.

What I will do is to maintain a central office and have individual managers that I will hold accountable. That's when I'll start cutting my work week down and maintain multiple residences. That will keep me challenged.

Has responsibility ever been an issue for you?

No. That's not even responsibility, that becomes more of a game. It takes money to make money, and once you start making more than you can use, it's just like playing monopoly.

You have a lot of self-confidence. How did you get to that point?

I believe in myself.

How do you balance between your professional and personal life in terms of being successful?

Well, I think behind every strong individual there is somebody in the shadows, whether that other person realizes it or not. I think that when things don't go well, you've got to complain to somebody, and it's probably the one who is the closest to you. I think that when everything is going real well, whoever you're with will share that as well. There's somebody behind the curtain.

What does it take to attain success?

I think most people want the world. They would love to drive big, pretty cars, and live in big, pretty homes; however, I don't think everyone is willing to do what it takes to get there. I guess the real answer to that question would be sacrifice and the ability to prepare themselves.

Does giving control to others come easy to you?

I can give control to others, as long as I can see them out of the corner of my eye. I need to know everything that involves the business so that I can intervene should the need arise.

Have you always been skilled at acquiring the knowledge to achieve your goals?

If one other person in the world knows, then it can be learned. Generally, it is at the tip of your fingers and you just don't know what to do. For instance, when I was interested in a franchise with McDonald's and Baskin-Robbins, I went to the library. They have information on microfilm. You just push up a title and every article that was ever printed comes up on microfilm. I just went and I Xeroxed everything that had to do with each company. So a lot of this information is right at the tip of your fingers.

With McDonald's, I flew around the country. I went to Seattle and other cities, and I found owners and cornered them, in a sense. It's hard to get individuals that will talk to you. Some of them wouldn't talk, but some of them did, and I got little bits and pieces.

You didn't give up?

Some of the obstacles that we go through just make us that much better of a person. I learned the hard way. I don't need a lot of help now. When you learn that way it costs you money, time, and headaches, and you're only going to mess up so much money.

You can take a person out of a setting, say some rich setting and put them in South Central LA. and they wouldn't last a day. But you could take someone out of the projects and give him a taste of the good life, and he's never going back. People from humble backgrounds actually have an advantage, I think. They have survival skills. They have experienced what it's like to have hard times, and they have something to strive for. Once you've had a little taste of success, you don't want to go back, because you know what going back is like. I think people from very comfortable backgrounds don't know what it is like to strive just to survive.

Are you a good steward with money?

It's not how much money you make, it's how much money you keep. I could make a lot of money, but if it costs me a lot to make it, then I haven't done anything. For example, take automobiles, when they made one they made another. It's not as if I have one of a kind or the only one in the world. Even with cars, I do my homework. I find out what it costs the manufacture and the dealer. Then I set the price that I will pay.

On a new car there are gas guzzler and luxury taxes that must be paid. There are one-time fees, and the first person who buys the car has to pay them. When I purchased my 500SL it had 4,000 miles on it. It hadn't been wrecked, so I wasn't concerned about the mileage. Plus, I had a four-year warranty and knew that Mercedes Benz would cover any problems.

What advice do you have for overcoming doubt, fear and procrastination?

We are our own worst enemy. You should have short-term and long-term goals. Once you achieve your goals, you must re-evaluate and start all over again. Life is like a series of deadlines. If you stop trying, then you cease to exist! As long as we believe in ourselves we can conquer anything.

Lisa Valore

A native Texan, Lisa Valore received her masters degree in Library Science at the age of 24. She has been working professionally in libraries since 1986. She has worked in many types of libraries during her tenure, including the Infomart Reference Library in Dallas Texas, the Texas Woman's University Library Science Library, The Duncanville Public Library, The Abilene Christian University Library, and currently she is the Branch Head of the South Ontario Branch Library in Ontario, California. Lisa and her husband Brent live in Brea, California, where they are the proud parents of three cats and two dogs. Lisa's primary goal in life is to share her love for people by helping them find what they need in the library setting.

Have doubt, fear and procrastination been major issues for you?

I use self-talk to help combat doubt, fear and procrastination. Half the time I'm thinking and saying,

"Okay, Lisa, just let it go, it's going to be all right, think it through." Then the other half of the time it's, "Oh, why am I so miserable?" If I feel defensive or get upset about something that is minimal, it is usually because I have self-doubts.

In my earlier school years procrastination was a problem for me. When I went to graduate school, it finally all clicked together. I had to hold down two jobs, plus take twelve hours of library school. It had to be done if I wanted a master's degree.

Some people say I'm too impulsive, because I will go ahead and finish the project, make the decision, do it, right or wrong, just to be able to get it out of my head, off my desk, and on to the next phase. If I have to revise, so be it.

Does faith play a tremendous part in overcoming your doubts and fears?

Faith and my sheer bullheadedness, which is, *I'm going to do this.* Yes, there are consequences, and I do think of the consequences before I act. However, just to be able to do something helps dispel the doubt and fear.

When it comes to these issues are your symptoms physical or psychological ?

Actually, I have both physical and psychological symptoms when I'm terribly worried about something. For example, my head itches and I'll be super nervous. I have to be constantly busy when I am worried and afraid about something, or I may turn into a zombie.

If it's dealing with my staff, asserting the authority that I have, and not feeling confident, then I have to say to myself, "Now think about this, you have earned the right to do this. You run a very good ship. Some people may have a different management style, but your style produces the happiest customers and a happier staff." When I do have to face a conflict, which is something that I detest, I get it over with quickly. That is my strength, I will not delay; I get it taken care of and let everyone heal.

When is procrastination healthy?

I don't put things off unless there is a conflict going on with a person who is very important to me, someone in my life whom I truly care about, such as a family member or a very close friend. I will postpone talking about the problem for no more than a week. I may need to gather my thoughts together, to be able to present whatever it is in the most loving, nurturing, and least conflicting manner possible. I really want to know the right words to say; plus, the situation may change without me having to say anything. If it's work-related and something that management needs to be aware of, I make sure I have established all of my facts, and have checked and re-checked. I wouldn't call that procrastination.

Are you good at giving control?

No, that's really hard for me. In my work and for the good of the library, I have to let go and let my employees make mistakes and grow. If I don't let them grow, I'm going to have morale problems, and a lot of miserable people. Once I let go of some things, it seems as if operations run much smoother.

There are certain things that I still can't delegate. When you are learning to delegate, you experience a backlash. You delegate everything to everybody and then say, "Hey, wait a minute, I don't have anything to do here." Once you find the balance, delegating is very useful and it really is best for the overall well-being of whatever organization you are in.

Overcoming Doubt, Fear and Procrastination

One of the reasons I decided to start delegating was because a staff member was feeling totally useless, and feeling left out. I got together with several other staff members and we discussed the problem and what we could do to make things better. So I delegated more responsibility to the person who felt left out.

Whether you have ten or 1,000 staff members, you have to be considerate of people's feelings. I delegate things to everyone to help them feel good about themselves, and to help the morale. I have delegated as much as I can without undermining my authority.

What has brought you a feeling of success?

I have been very successful in my career. I majored in English in college and didn't do very well. My mom was a school librarian, and so I thought I would give that a try. I graduated from college. I was put on probation in graduate school. Then something clicked. I believe with the Lord's help, I made it to every class. I took a lot of notes and held down two jobs. Out of 36 hours of courses, I earned a B in two classes, and earned an A in all of the other classes. For me to go from one extreme to another was a success. I learned that I have the capability to do what needs to be done.

What advice do you have for overcoming doubt, fear and procrastination?

Take that first step. Be organized in your life and write lists of things-to-do, with the attitude that yes, this is going to work for me—I'm going to do it. Organize all of your paperwork and your files. Put on the appearance of confidence, even if you don't have a lick of it. Just do the best you can; and when you've done the best you can, don't worry about it anymore. That may sound trite, but it works.

Gail Taylor Walton

Born in Texas and raised in the Los Angeles area, Gail Taylor Walton graduated from Washington High School in Los Angeles. Being acutely aware of her limited formal education, Gail knew she would always have to go beyond basic job expectations in order to achieve status as a valued, sought-after employee. She did this by becoming a voracious reader, taking educational classes as her schedule permitted, and absorbing all of the knowledge those around her were willing to share. Gradually, while sometimes maintaining three jobs simultaneously and meeting the demands of single parenthood, she began to ascend through the ranks.

In 1969, Gail began what would ultimately be a long career in administrative work in the health care field. She took an instant liking to the work and found herself in the midst of some very educated and kind professionals who recognized her as dependable, hardworking and effective. Her most recent position was program coordinator for a physician training program.

Overcoming Doubt, Fear and Procrastination

With the support of family and friends, Gail overcame the personal demons borne of a devastating tragedy early in her adult life to emerge a woman with a healthy self-respect that had previously eluded her throughout most of her life. At present, Gail resides with her husband and daughter in Redondo Beach, California. She currently runs her own medical transcription service, _Operative Words._ In her spare time, she likes to write and study human behavior.

Gail is overly modest about her many achievements and accomplishments in life, but she has a wonderful philosophy: "It's not what you do, but how well you do it. There can be integrity in any job done well."

Do you have any fears?

One of my ongoing fears is that I'll lose my temper. I never know when it's going to happen. It's one of the things that I really don't have any more control over than I had when I was a young girl.

Have you conquered doubt and fear?

I have been successful at overcoming a lot of doubt about myself. I've overcome doubts about humanity in general. I used to be extremely cynical. Living a number of years and going through some rough times I found out that people can be kind. They can be good, gentle, supportive and understanding. It's made me a better and more confident person now that I'm able to accept people more.

Have you ever felt like a failure?

Yes. Many times. Most of my life, especially the younger portion. Why I felt like a failure, I really can't tell you. And I'm glad that I can't tell you, because that is an indication to me that I have managed to pretty much abolish that trait in myself. I would wake up in the morning feeling like a failure, and would go to bed in the evening feeling like a failure.

How did you overcome the feeling?

I had the good fortune of being exposed to some very patient people who showed me just by their example of how people can be, how life can be, and what my capabilities are. They didn't try to push me; they guided me, and let me see that I am a worthwhile person. I was put into situations where I had to do some things that I considered difficult to face, and over my head. And I did them. My confidence started to grow once I realized that I had managed these things. The feelings of inadequacy and failure just gradually diminished. I don't have those feelings anymore. When you see yourself doing something that you didn't think you could (notice I said *doing* something), you don't even have to complete it, necessarily, but if you face it, walk up to it, start it, and get involved in it, you feel better than if you had hidden under a rock someplace and waited for whatever it was to go away and take care of itself.

In my profession I always go the extra mile. I don't do just enough to get by. I always add my own touches. I do my homework, I do my research, and I'm conscientious. I give whatever I'm doing all that I have. I'm not casual about anything, because, as much as I hate clichés, some of those old sayings are true. For example, *a job worth doing is worth doing well.* I honestly believe that. People pick that up about me. They trust me; they find me reliable. This makes me successful.

Are you good at giving control to others?

I'm working on that. I don't know what that stems from. Maybe it extends from being an only child and always being in control. When you grow up as an only child, nothing much happens that you don't make happen. Nothing gets misplaced that you didn't personally misplace, nothing gets broken that you didn't personally break, especially when you are an only child who doesn't even have a pet. Once a friend told me that it's good for children to have a pet because that is something that they cannot control, and they start learning to deal with things that they can't control.

Giving control to others bothers me. It's one of my weaknesses at my job, and I've been told that repeatedly. I know I don't delegate much. I'm trying, and I'm getting better at it, because I keep reminding myself that somebody had to trust me and I'm trying to pass that along. I know that it does make people feel good to be given more responsibility. So I'm working on it.

Do you allow others to assign value or self-worth to you?

Only if it's good. Only if it works to my advantage. I can pick out the parts that I like. I kick out the rest, because it would be too devastating not to. If I'm being criticized, then I'll seek a second opinion, somebody whom I respect. If it is an irrational type of put-down or someone questioning my integrity or my ability, then I don't accept that.

What makes you accept or disregard advice from people?

With me, it is mostly the spirit in which it is given; it is the circumstance that brought it about and it is that person's track record. When you are giving advice in certain areas, you need to make sure that at least those areas of your own house are clean. So that's what I look at. I consider the source, and take it from there.

Do you need the approval or acceptance of a loved one in order to proceed with your goals?

No, I don't need that, but admittedly it helps; it makes a difference. It doesn't have to be an overwhelming approval and doesn't have to be an extremely strong acceptance. If the approval or acceptance is strong, then that shoots me right into outer-space with whatever it is I'm thinking of doing, but it's not absolutely necessary. When you are an only child, you get used to acting autonomously.

Are you a perfectionist?

I have been told that I am a perfectionist. Since having been told that, I do see it in myself. I don't have any patience with myself when it comes to making errors, which is unrealistic. I aim for perfection and I expect perfection. I need to focus on not going absolutely bananas when the results turn out to be less than perfect.

When do you feel bad about yourself?

Oh, that's easy. I feel bad about myself when I lose my infamous temper. I have a really tragic temper. It doesn't come up much, but it comes and I don't like that.

When do you especially feel good about yourself?

I feel especially good about myself when I do something that I didn't think that I could do, even if I'm pretty much forced to do it. If I do something that would normally require several hours, and I get it done in 45 minutes to meet a deadline, I feel great. To meet deadlines and face difficult things brings a feeling of great satisfaction to me. I get a natural *high* when I do something for someone else. That's when I really feel good. It doesn't even have to be a big thing. It can just be seeing elderly people at the bus stop and giving them a ride to wherever they need to go. It just really feels good to help people. I can't think of anything else that feels better. It's something that even as a child I always did. I have been especially considerate of older people, and sticking up for people who were handicapped or physically challenged.

I feel happy being an independent thinker and reaching my own decisions despite popular opinion. Those types of things make me feel more in control; they make me feel like somebody who can't be bought or sold. I have integrity. It's one of the few things that I tend to flash, like a peacock. With some women, it's their legs, their eyes, and their good looks. With me, I like the fact that I can't be bought.

Connie Amaden-Crawford

Connie Amaden-Crawford is a fashion specialist, educator, and author whose 26 year career spans everything from fashion designer to pattern-maker, grader and design consultant.

Ms. Crawford has been a guest speaker on ABC's TV series *Home*. She has also been a guest lecturer for various fashion seminars, colleges, and women's organizations. She is a published author of four textbooks, *A Guide to Fashion Sewing, The Art of Fashion Draping, Fashion Your own Pants the Simple Way,* and *Fashion Your Own Skirts the Simple Way.*

Ms. Crawford has recently been employed as the education coordinator for Bonfit America, Inc. During this special assignment, she wrote pattern-making and sewing instructional books for Bonfit.

Connie also teaches full time at the Fashion Institute of Design and Merchandising in Los Angeles, California. She has taught there for 21 years. Recently, Ms. Crawford wrote a grading workbook and a computer workbook for the Fashion Institute to help students learn grading and computer pattern making.

Connie Amaden-Crawford, like many Americans, had a fear of flying. Being a high-profile individual traveling and making personal appearances, she has to fly. When you have no alternative but to face your fear, how do you get over it? In this interview she shares how she got over the fear of flying.

Connie, how did you get to the point where you were no longer afraid to fly?

Oh, after the plane crash. I've never told you about....

She pauses for a moment. Remembering the ordeal, she becomes emotional. Sensing her need to be consoled, I stopped the recorder to comfort her, she regains her composure. I asked her, "Are you sure you want to talk about this?"

Yes. In 1978 I was in a plane crash. I was single and dating a wealthy boyfriend at the time. We had taken a six-seater Cessna airplane to Sacramento. We were flying back to Burbank, ready to land and were in the area of Van Nuys. Have you ever been in a small plane? You can hear everything the pilot and co-pilot say. All of sudden we were over Van Nuys and the pilot yelled to the co-pilot, "I can't hold it! I can't hold it!" as he was yawing into the ground.

Being raised as a good Roman Catholic girl, I remembered that I was supposed to say some prayers and the Act of Contrition. They say that if you say it at the time of death, you will go directly to Heaven.

I figured I didn't have enough time to say a prayer—it's a long prayer. I was strapped in my seat belt and it was getting tighter. I said to God, "Well, if this is when you want me, then you may have me." A feeling of total peace came over me, as a big, bright light came and engulfed me. We ended up crashing. We hit a dirt lot before we hit the airport. We bounced and hit the right side; the wing and the engine tore off; we continued to bounce to the left side, and that wing and engine tore off, as well. The plane turned around, and the nose tore off. It ended when we came around and hit a chain link fence, which tore off the tail of the plane.

I was in the only place in the plane that was left in tact. I was totally unhurt. I should have died in that plane crash. The pilot and co-pilot lived, but it took five hours to sew up their heads and take care of their broken bones. They were pretty mutilated, but they lived.

Because I was okay, nobody even wanted to look at me. When I got to the hospital they were so busy sewing up the pilots, they just let me sit there. Finally, five hours later, they said, "You can go home." I said, "Why don't you take my blood pressure or something, just for insurance reasons." They took my blood pressure and found out it was 40 over 60. I should have been dead. It was my way of going into shock. Well, they panicked. They thought I had internal bleeding, because the seat belt had literally touched my backbone. They tested me and I had no internal bleeding, so they let me go home.

I started reading books—two, three, or four books a week—about life after death, spiritual things, all kinds of religions. The plane crash helped me get over my fear of flying. I went home and I've been fine ever since, no problems. No fear of flying!

About the Author

It is as if Barbara Wright Sykes were destined to write *Overcoming Doubt, Fear, and Procrastination*. Her life is written like a novel, with the theme of overcoming obstacles such as doubt, fear, and procrastination woven through each chapter. Success has not come easy for Barbara, but with her determination, drive, and strong belief-system, she has worked tirelessly to climb and reach each step of success as a wife and mother, devoted Christian, business entrepreneur, and as a writer and speaker.

Barbara worked hard and sacrificed much to obtain two college degrees, one in accounting and a second in business education, with an emphasis in marketing. For a decade, she owned *Elegance In Vogue*, a clothing store located in Hawthorne, California. She formerly taught college in such disciplines as business, psychology and career development, for which she received an Outstanding Teacher Award.

Overcoming the Obstacles—The Real Story

Barbara is an accomplished public speaker, and can often be seen as a featured guest speaker at seminars. She travels throughout the year making personal appearances on radio and television. There have been numerous articles written about her; most notably the _Los Angeles Times_, _Income Opportunity_, and _Health Magazine_.

Barbara writes feature articles for a number of national magazines, and she has written a business textbook and recorded an audio album aimed at designers, tailors and sewing professionals entitled, _The "Business" of Sewing_. In addition to her busy schedule she is also senior editor of a newsletter of the same name.

She is a business consultant and consults under her firm's name, Barbara Wright and Associates. Ms. Wright Sykes consults with professionals who either want to go into business or who are already in business and experiencing difficulties. These real life situations have enhanced her ability to develop techniques encouraging and promoting positive thoughts and productive attitudes that have guided individuals through some troubled times. Thus, she has addressed those issues in her seminars and now, in this book, _Overcoming Doubt, Fear and Procrastination._

Barbara inspires people with her down-to-earth wisdom, as she guides individuals to their life-long goals. Her motto, "Determination equals Success!" encourages individuals to look forward to the personal and spiritual satisfaction that life has to offer. Barbara Wright Sykes has been appreciated and recognized for her hard work and dedication to others. Those who know her well, speak highly of her:

Overcoming Doubt, Fear and Procrastination

Barbara does everything with her whole heart and soul. Her enthusiasm is catching, as she straps on her boots, rolls up her sleeves, and tackles the "to do" list before her. She is sincere in wanting to help others, which is evident as she addresses her readers and her audience at the various seminars and speaking engagements in which she shares her many secrets and how-tos of success.

—**Katie Mead**

Barbara is one of the most consistent people I have ever met; consistent in that she is a goal-oriented, people-person, with an enormous amount of energy for others. That element accounts for a big part of her success. In spite of her success, she remains down-to-earth.

Barbara has a unique talent for expressing appreciation for the accomplishments of others. As a result, other successful people have taken notice of her sincerity, and are fed by her energy.

Barbara knows how to embrace the positive and withhold birth from that which is negative. I recall, a while ago, having discussed with Barbara the details of a business enterprise which did not work out. I will forever remember and value her ability to listen well and respond within the context of my experience. I have learned much by observing Barbara in action. It is impossible to know her without experiencing a wealth of energy and enthusiasm. If you're going someplace in life, you will want to know Barbara Wright Sykes. She is a winner.

—**S. Barry Hamdani**

Appendix

Books/Bibliography

Blacklash, Cecil C. Whiting, PhD, California.

Beyond Fear, Robert Handly, New York, Rawson Associates, 1987.

History of Modern Psychology, New York, Academic Press, 1989.

How to Conquer Your Fears, Phobias, and Anxieties, Herbert Fensterheim, Greens Farms, Connecticut, Wildcat Publishing Company, 1995 (Revised edition of *Stop Running Scared!*, 1977).

Procrastination: Why You Do It, What To Do About It, Jane B. Burka and Lenora M. Yuen, Massachusetts, Addison Wesley Publishing Company, 1983.

Psychotherapy by Reciprocal Intervention, Joseph Wolpe, Stanford, Stanford University Press, 1971.

Secrets of Personal Marketing Power, Don L. Price, Iowa, Kendall/Hunt Publishing Company, 1994.

Show Me How To Love You: Creating Your Own Couples Support Group, Jane Meyers Drew, PhD, California, 1996.

Tales of Tichuba, Cecil C. Whiting, PhD, California.

The Roots of Religious Doubt and the Search for Security, New York, Seabury Press, 1974.

Where Were You When I Needed You Dad?: A Guide For Healing Your Father Wound, Jane Meyers Drew, PhD, California, 1992.

Index

Index

loneliness, 25
loud noises, 24
marriage, 25
rejection, 23, 25, 130, 161
relationships, 25
responsibility, 25
snakes, 21
success, 25, 82-98, 142
swimming, 25
water, 25
weight, 25
world conditions, 191
Filtering Process, 70
Five-Step Approach, 11, 12
Food For Thought, 9
Frame of Reference, 6, 25, 65, 84
Frank Works Through the Problem, 7
Frank's Arsenal of Excuses, 55
Functional Autonomy, 142, 143

G

George, Warren, 89-94
Goals, 57, 60, 61, 62, 86, 88,
Giving control, 73-79, 108, 123,
134, 163, 189, 202, 208, 213, 217
Guilt, 9, 43-54, 75
    healthy 46-50
    motivational, 46
    origin, 50
    unhealthy, 54

H

Hamdani, S. Barry, 32, 37, 42, 87,
154-159
Higher Spiritual Power, 138, 203

I

Interpersonal Relationships, 26,35, 68, 76
Introspection, 19

J

Jackson, Jesse, 103
James, William, 17
Jesus Christ, 37, 173, 203
Joyner, Florence Griffith, 106

L

Leadership, 76, 79-81, 151

communication, 80
confidence, 80, 81
delegating, 79-81
fear of, 81
mentoring, 81
respect, 80
LearnKey, 99, 114-126, 173, 174
Lee, Spike, 112
Lord, 168

M

Manipulation, 73, 75
Meichembaum, Donald, 17, 19
Multiphasic Personality Test, 145

N

Negative, 10, 32, 38, 46, 96,
Networking, 86, 87, 104
New You, The, 96, 97
"No Principle" Exercise, 94-96
Noxious Environmental Stimuli, 16
Noxious Stimuli, 21

O

Opinion(s), 9, 69, 70, 109, 135, 142,
Overcoming the Obstacles, 11, 15,
    see doubt, fear and procrastination

P

Passion, 84, 86, 146
Peale, Norman Vincent, 17
Peer Pressure, 51-53, 68
Perfection, 45, 58-61, 110, 165, 200
Perfectionist(s), 58-61, 135, 152, 158,
161, 219
Permission, 68, 82, 84
    dependency, 84, 94
    giving yourself, 84, 94
    procrastinate, 83
    reinforcement, 85
    superiority, 94, 96
    validate, 82
Personal Empowerment, 186
Personality Tests, 145, 184
Pierce, Roberta, 37, 88, 147
Positive Thinking Exercise, 18
Praise Factor, 67,151, 152
Price, Don. L., 86, 87, 186-191
Priorities, 86. 88,90, 182

Index

YOU'LL LOVE OUR RELATED PRODUCTS!

*The following dynamic tools and articles will inspire
and motivate you on a daily basis to reach success!*

1. *Overcoming Doubt, Fear and Procrastination Workbook:* Now you can work each day and chart your progress in overcoming the demons that have kept you from living the happy, productive life that you deserve!

2. *Overcoming Doubt, Fear and Procrastination CD-ROM:* Through modern technology, the keys to opening the doors of success are literally at your finger-tips!

3. *Overcoming Doubt, Fear and Procrastination audio:* Listen and be inspired as you travel to and from work, armed with determination and the principles needed to succeed!

4. *Overcoming Doubt, Fear and Procrastination video:* Barbara Wright Sykes will come into your home as often as you need her, to inspire and motivate you to new heights of success! With her guiding and cheering you on, there's no stopping you now!

5. Tee-shirts, mugs, and plaques containing a picture and/or inscription of one of the following:

*The book cover of Overcoming Doubt, Fear and Procrastination
The New You
You Might Be a Procrastinator If....
The Procrastinator's Oath*

You can be reinforced, drink to your success, and even advertise the fact that you are overcoming doubt, fear and procrastination, and that you are a special person who deserves peace and happiness. These are great gifts for friends, loved ones, and the office staff! If you're unsure of their needs and likes, give a gift of love by giving a gift certificate! For information about these great products, call the toll-free number, 1-800-795-8999.